Sports and food are inextricably linked. ... uper Bowl parties, hot dogs, the local pub, and r... 'l part of enjoying the spectacle of a game, ...me.

When it comes to football, thoroug... ...g goes into the preparation of the perfect tailgate party, or viewing party from home. The serious football fan must have a spread that demonstrates both his or her commitment to the team, but also satisfies that base need of delicious food.

Our goal with this cookbook is to provide inspiration to fans who want to take their next party up a notch. With recipes inspired by each team of pro football, you'll be able to throw a party with dishes that perfectly compliment the combatants of the big game.

We present 96 versatile recipes that can be prepared at home or at a tailgate party, with an entrée, appetizer, and cocktail inspired by each team and region of pro football. If your team is playing Baltimore, try making the crab cakes with purple Poe-tatoes. How about classic lobster rolls for when your team takes on the Patriots? Or BBQ when your team plays Carolina?

You'll have several seasons worth of ideas, and will instantly be the most popular tailgate master. Your house will become the place to be on Sundays. Your game day just got that much better.

Enjoy the journey!

Pro Football Cookbook: Recipes for Home or the Tailgate

Copyright© 2013 by Paul Swaney, Stadium Journey LLC

Stadium Photo Credits: Daniel Armstrong, Jason Bartel, Blake Benzel, Drew Cieszynski, Geoff Crawley, Paul Donaldson, Jim Folsom, Christopher Green, Jack Harver, Gary Herman, Kevin Kelley, Conrad Klank, Andrew Kulyk, Rich Kurtzman, Sean MacDonald, Dennis Morrell, Ryan Norris, Aaron Novinger, Michael Spatz, Hans Steiniger, Paul Swaney, Tom Uddo, Jack Winter, and Daniel Wolf

Requests for permission to make copies of any part of the work should be submitted online at info@mascotbooks.com or mailed to Mascot Books, 560 Herndon Parkway #120, Herndon, VA 20170.

PRT1013A

Printed in the United States

ISBN-13: 9781620865033
ISBN-10: 1620865033

www.mascotboks.com

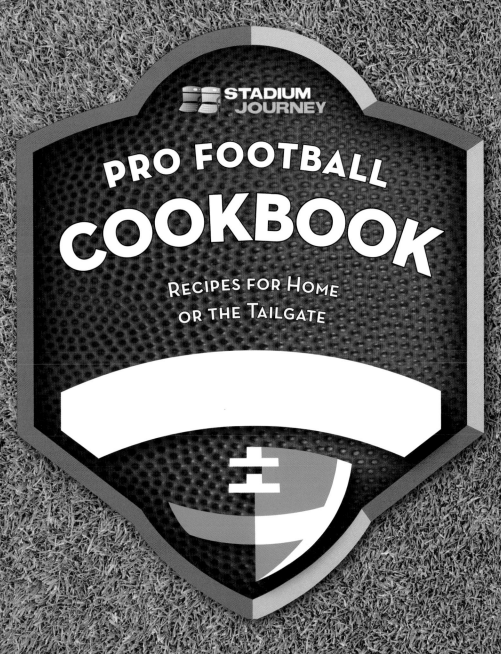

PRO FOOTBALL
COOKBOOK

Recipes for Home
or the Tailgate

TABLE OF CONTENTS

PRO FOOTBALL
COOKBOOK
RECIPES FOR HOME
OR THE TAILGATE

ARIZONA

ANCHO CHILE AND COFFEE RUBBED TRI-TIP OF BEEF

Submission by Christopher Crump

. . . .

What is tri-tip? Originally a California cut, this steak has become increasingly popular because of the superior flavor and its perfect structure for grilling. The tri-tip steak is a triangular section of the sirloin primal and comes to a point where the sirloin meets the round and flank primals. I love using this steak for its intense flavor, because it is far less expensive than other steaks, and because of the excellent marbling and tenderness, as long as it is not overcooked. Serve with your favorite taco accessories such as avocado, sour cream, grilled vegetables, cilantro, or pico de gallo. Serves 10-12

. . . .

INGREDIENTS:

3 pounds tri-tip beef roast

1 tbsp vegetable oil

Tortillas for serving

RUB:

⅓ cup kosher coarse sea salt

¾ cup fresh ground coffee

¼ cup smoked paprika

¼ cup light brown sugar

4 tbsp ancho chile powder

2 tbsp ground cumin

4 tbsp cracked black pepper

1. Pre-heat a grill over medium-high heat.

2. Combine ingredients for the rub in a small mixing bowl.

3. Rub tri-tip with an even coat of vegetable oil. Generously coat beef with the rub.

4. Place steak on the grill for 8-10 minutes per side, or until the meat reaches an internal temperature of 130 degrees for medium rare.

5. Remove from heat and allow to rest for 10-15 minutes.

6. Slice steaks across the grain and serve with grilled tortillas and selected condiments.

DESERT ROASTED CORN ON THE COB WITH AGAVE-LIME BUTTER AND QUESO FRESCO

This corn on the cob brings true desert flavor to your tailgate party. It's sweet, sour, savory, and grilled. Best of all, there are no utensils required. Serves 8

INGREDIENTS:

8 ears of corn in the husk

3 limes

1 cup queso fresco

1 pound unsalted butter

2 ounces agave nectar

1 tbsp chili powder

Salt and pepper

1. Soak corn in water for 15 minutes (up to 2 hours before grilling), place corn on grill in husk for 30 minutes, rotating every 5-10 minutes until lightly charred inside.

2. Meanwhile, zest and juice the limes and combine with butter, agave nectar, and chili powder in a small pot and place on the grill until butter is melted.

3. Remove corn from grill and pull off the husk. Brush the corn with butter mixture, and salt and pepper. Garnish with queso fresco.

I am the owner/chef of Nomad Catering located in Scottsdale, Arizona. Nomad Catering was started in 2009 after my many culinary journeys through North and Central America. Through my travels, there were three main things that I had always carried with me: my passion for food, beverages, and sports. I have a culinary and hospitality background of over 20 years ranging from regional casual cuisine to Five Diamond fine dining. On my nomadic travels, it has always been my purpose to learn, support, and embrace the local culture and cuisine.

I have always had a huge passion for competition and sports. I have found that no matter where I go or what I may be doing, I could always pull up a barstool, engage in the endless banter of the local sports team, sip on the local grog, and indulge in the amazing regional recipes that our country has to offer.

-Christopher Crump

THE JAVELINA

A spicy twist on a favorite south of the border cocktail. Makes 1 cocktail

INGREDIENTS:

2 ounces silver tequila

1 ½ ounces pineapple juice

½ ounce agave nectar

½ ounce triple sec

½ ounce fresh squeezed lime juice (about ½ a lime)

1 slice fresh jalapeño

1. In a cocktail shaker, muddle the sliced jalapeño.

2. Add tequila, pineapple juice, agave nectar, triple sec, and lime juice.

3. Shake vigorously and strain over ice.

4. Garnish with slice of pineapple, lime, or jalapeño.

"DIRTY BIRD" CHICKEN

Submission by Christopher Crump

. . . .

Brining is one of my favorite techniques for inducing flavor and moisture into meat. By brining, your meat will be less likely to dry out and will be much more tender. This bold peach-brined chicken will make any running back dance. Serves 8-10

. . . .

INGREDIENTS:

24 pieces of chicken (legs, thighs, and wings)

4 fresh peaches, pitted and chopped

2 chipotle peppers with adobo sauce from can

½ cup diced white onion

½ cup ketchup

2 tbsp apple cider vinegar

½ cup peach ale (substitute beer if you can't find peach ale)

2 tbsp light brown sugar

3 cloves garlic, crushed

2 tbsp smoked paprika

4 jalapeños, sliced

1 cup soy sauce

3 bay leaves

2 cans of peaches with syrup

1 yellow onion, chopped

3 tbsp butter

6 quarts cold water

1. Brine the chicken. Combine water, chicken, canned peaches, jalapeños, soy sauce, and bay leaves in a large container and refrigerate for at least 12 hours. It is best if you do this a day in advance or the night before the big game.

2. In a large sauté pan, melt the butter over medium heat. Cook onion and fresh peaches until almost translucent. Add garlic and cook for an additional minute.

3. Add peach ale and cook for 5 minutes to reduce.

4. Add ketchup, vinegar, paprika, chipotle, adobo, and light brown sugar. Cook for 30 minutes on low/simmer.

5. Meanwhile, pre-heat a grill to medium-high.

6. Remove from heat and blend with an immersion blender or in a food processor.

7. Strain in a bowl and refrigerate before serving.

8. Remove chicken from brine and pat dry with a paper towel.

9. Place chicken on grill on medium-high heat, skin side down.

10. Grill for about 10 minutes until light caramelization begins.

11. Flip chicken and continue to grill until internal temperature reaches 165 degrees.

12. Heat BBQ sauce on the grill until it reaches a simmer.

13. Remove chicken from grill and dip each piece in the BBQ sauce and serve.

SHRIMP AND GRITS WITH ANDOUILLE

A modern take on an iconic southern dish. Make the compound butter and polenta the night before the game at home. Serves 12

INGREDIENTS:

1 pound unsalted butter (at room temperature)

2 large lemons

1 box of quick polenta (preferably cheese or fresh herb)

1 cup extra virgin olive oil

4 cloves garlic, crushed

1 bunch fresh thyme

2 pounds Gulf shrimp, peeled and de-veined (16-20 count)

2 tbsp honey

4 smoked Andouille sausage links

Salt and pepper

1. The day before the game, make lemon compound butter.

2. Combine butter, zest, and juice from two lemons, salt, and pepper. Whip to combine and place in refrigerator for up to 24 hours in advance.

3. Follow instructions to make polenta on the box (make up to 12 hours in advance).

4. Pour polenta on a baking sheet and spread evenly.

5. Place in refrigerator so it can cool and firm up, about 2-3 hours. Cut into square 2-inch pieces. If tailgating, this can be done the day before.

6. Combine garlic, olive oil, thyme, honey, salt, and pepper. Mix well and add shrimp. Allow to marinate for 20-30 minutes.

7. Meanwhile, pre-heat a grill to medium.

8. Place Andouille sausage on the grill, rotating every few minutes until the internal temperature reaches 165 degrees.

9. Place polenta squares on the grill and cook for 5 minutes. Flip and cook for an additional 5 minutes.

10. After the flipping the polenta, add shrimp to the grill and cook about 3 minutes per side until pink.

11. Remove sausage from grill and slice.

12. On a serving platter, assemble the polenta squares with three slices of sausage and three shrimp on each square. Top each square with 1 tbsp of compound butter.

GEORGIA MULE

An American version of a Moscow Mule. This cocktail brings all the flavors of the South to your tailgating party. Makes 1 cocktail

INGREDIENTS:

2 ounces rye whisky (preferably Bulleit Rye)

2 ounces ginger beer (preferably Gosling's brand)

1 ounce peach syrup

½ lime

Sprig of mint

1. In a cocktail shaker, add whisky, ginger beer, peach syrup, and lime (squeeze in lime juice, then add the lime to the mix).

2. Shake vigorously and strain over ice into a cocktail glass.

3. Garnish with mint spring.

BALTIMORE

MARYLAND CRAB CAKES WITH PURPLE SLAW

Submission by Paul Swaney

···

It doesn't get much better than a big crab cake on a crisp Sunday afternoon. This recipe keeps the crab lightly dressed so the crab taste can shine through. If tailgating, you should consider bringing a pan with you as these cakes can easily fall through the grates on the grill. Makes 6 large crab cakes

···

INGREDIENTS:

Crab Cakes:

1 pound crab (lump or backfin crab, or a combination)

¼ cup mayonnaise

1 egg

1 tsp Dijon mustard

1 tsp lemon juice

½ tsp Worcestershire sauce

1 tsp Old Bay seasoning

½ tsp salt

¼ tsp black pepper

1 ½ tbsp finely chopped fresh parsley

½ cup dried bread crumbs

2 tbsp butter

1 tbsp olive oil

Purple Slaw:

1 head red cabbage

1 lime, juiced

1 tbsp olive oil

¼ tsp salt

¼ tsp pepper

1. Drain crab and pick through to remove any pieces of shell. Place in a large mixing bowl.

2. In a medium bowl, beat the egg and then mix in the mayonnaise, mustard, lemon juice, Worcestershire sauce, Old Bay, salt, and pepper. Pour over crab, and mix very gently as to not break up the crab.

3. Add parsley and bread crumbs to mixture, and mix gently again. You should have a loose mixture. Cover and refrigerate for 1-3 hours.

4. To make the slaw, slice half the head of cabbage into thin slices. Place in a small bowl and cover with lime juice, olive oil, salt, and pepper. Mix well and let marinate while you cook the crab cakes, then serve on the side.

5. Remove crab mixture and shape into patties about the size of the palm of your hand.

6. In a large pan, melt the butter over medium heat and add the olive oil. When butter is bubbling, add crab cakes and cook 5 minutes. Flip carefully and cook another 5 minutes. Serve with side of slaw.

EDGAR ALLAN
PURPLE POE-TATOES

The Baltimore Ravens were named in homage to American author Edgar Allan Poe, a native of Baltimore. His narrative poem, "The Raven," published in 1845, is the inspiration for the team's name. This easy side dish is a festive way to celebrate a Ravens game. Serves 6

INGREDIENTS:

2 pounds of purple potatoes (substitute other small potatoes if you can't find the purple ones, but you lose some of the festivity of the dish)

½ red onion, sliced

⅓ cup olive oil

½ tsp Old Bay seasoning

½ tsp cayenne pepper (optional)

½ tsp dried thyme

¼ tsp salt

1. Pre-heat grill or oven to 425 degrees.

2. Cut potatoes into uniform bite-sized quarters and place in a medium bowl.

3. Add remaining ingredients and mix well.

4. Place in a grill basket if grilling, or on a baking sheet and roast for 40 minutes, or until fork-tender.

I founded Stadium Journey in 2009 out of a love of sports and travel, but the truth is that I am a foodie at heart and love to cook. When I'm not on the road, I am often in the kitchen or at the grill preparing food for my wife and son, or hosting friends and family.

-Paul Swaney

THE RAVEN

A strong purplish-black cocktail that is perfect for a Ravens game day party.

Makes 1 cocktail

INGREDIENTS:

¼ cup vodka

¼ cup white rum

¼ cup black raspberry liqueur (I like Chateau Monet, or Chambord)

1 ½ ounces blue curacao

3 blackberries for garnish (with a toothpick)

1. Fill a cocktail shaker with ice and add the liquid ingredients. Shake vigorously and strain into a martini glass.

2. Garnish by skewering blackberries on a toothpick and hanging from the edge of the glass.

BUFFALO

BUFFALO BACON BREAKFAST SLIDERS

Submission by Chris Tokarski

....

In Buffalo, the tailgating starts early, so it is appropriate to go for a breakfast slant on these recipes. Bison meat is found in most stores, but if you have to you can substitute hamburger for this recipe. Makes 6 sliders

....

INGREDIENTS:

1 pound ground bison

6 slices of thick-cut bacon

1 tbsp finely chopped fresh thyme (use half as much if you used dried thyme, substitute sage if needed)

¾ tsp salt

1 tsp fresh ground pepper

6 eggs

1 tbsp butter

6 slices cheddar cheese

6 small pretzel rolls (substitute English muffins or another small roll)

1. Fry bacon in a large pan or skillet.

2. Place bacon on a paper towel lined plate to soak up extra grease. Reserve 2 tsp of bacon fat for cooking the potatoes (recipe to follow).

3. Mix together bison, salt, pepper, and thyme.

4. Make 6 small burger patties from the bison, leave a small depression in the middle of each patty to prevent patties from bulging at the center during cooking.

5. Grill or pan-fry bison patties, 3-4 minutes per side for medium rare.

6. Remove patties from grill and cover with foil.

7. Heat frying pan on medium heat. Add butter and heat until butter melts.

8. Cook eggs in frying pan, place cheese slices on top when eggs are nearly cooked through, allowing 1-2 minutes for cheese to melt.

9. Place bison patties on buns and top with a half slice of bacon, fried egg, and cheese.

BREAKFAST POTATOES

....

A hearty and easy to make side dish, providing plenty of sustenance to get you through game day. Serves 6

....

INGREDIENTS:

5 medium red potatoes

2 tsp bacon fat (substitute butter if needed)

2 tbsp butter

1 red onion, chopped

Salt and pepper

1. Place potatoes in a large stockpot. Fill pot with water, covering potatoes. Heat pot over high heat.

2. While water is heating, heat 2 tsp of reserved bacon fat in a large frying pan. Cook onions over medium heat until they are lightly caramelized. Remove onions from pan.

3. Cook potatoes until fork tender, about 10-15 minutes after water boils. Drain potatoes in a colander.

4. After potatoes have cooled until you can handle, dice them into bite-sized chunks.

5. Melt butter over medium heat in a large frying pan. Cook potatoes until crisp and brown, about 15 minutes.

6. Season potatoes with salt and pepper. Add in onions and cook for an additional 2-3 minutes and serve.

BEERMOSA

....

It may sound strange if you have never tried it, but this is the perfect morning cocktail to compliment your recipes. Makes 1 cocktail

....

INGREDIENTS:

Orange juice

Your favorite India Pale Ale

1. Fill a champagne flute half full with orange juice. Fill the remaining space with beer. Repeat as necessary.

I fell in love with the Bills during their Super Bowl XXV loss, and tragically continue to root for them to this day. I also ably coached Thurman Thomas to a 5,236-yard rushing season in Super Tecmo Bowl.

-Chris Tokarski

CAROLINA

NORTH CAROLINA SMOKED SPARE RIBS

Submission by Anna Hopkins

....

Smoked, tender spare ribs with a salty rub. Perfect as is or slathered in a vinegary BBQ sauce. Consider applying the rub the night before the big game. Serves 2 (multiply depending on the size of your party)

....

INGREDIENTS:

1 rack pork spare ribs (about 2 pounds)

½ cup dry rub (see recipe below)

Charcoal

1 pack smoker chips

RUB:

¼ cup salt

⅓ cup dark brown sugar

3 tbsp + 1 tsp chili powder

1 tbsp cayenne pepper

2 tbsp paprika

½ tsp allspice

1 tbsp dried oregano

1 tbsp + 1 tsp black pepper

1 tbsp garlic salt

1 tbsp cumin

HOW TO MAKE YOUR OWN SMOKER

Supplies Needed:
- Grill
- Charcoal briquettes
- Smoker Wood Chips (hickory or whatever flavor you'd like)
- Foil
- Grill or oven thermometer
- Charcoal Barrel Starter (not necessary but helps tremendously)

Method:
- Soak your wood chips (read package).
- Start charcoal in charcoal barrel starter. Once top coals begin to turn gray, place hot coals on one half of grill.
- Put soaked wood chips in tin foil, fold shut, and place several slits in top to allow smoke to escape out.
- Place foil wood chip packet on top of hot coals, then put grill grate down, and allow chips to smoke and grate to get hot (3-7 minutes).
- Once grate is hot and chips are smoking, place meat on opposite side of hot coals. Open vents on bottom of grill to half open, top to half as well, adjust as needed to regulate heat.
- A good smoke temperature is about 215-260 degrees depending on the length of time you are smoking. Generally, to achieve an intense smoke flavor, remember the saying "low and slow" referring to low temperature and a lengthy cook time.
- Add new coals to old coals when old coals start to fade (after an hour or so, leave lid open to allow new coals to get lit). Meat is done when it is cooked through and reads the proper temperature, depending on the item, and is tender.

Continues on next page

1. Combine rub ingredients and rub generously all over ribs. Refrigerate for 12-24 hours.

2. Prepare your smoker by following guidelines for "At Home Smoker".

3. Place ribs on the grill. To ensure a consistent smoking temperature of about 225 degrees, check on your ribs every 30 minutes. After 2 hours, pick up the ribs in the center with your grill tongs. You are looking for the ribs to bend and form a nice horseshoe shape—but not falling apart. This is a good indicator that the ribs are tender and nearly finished. Once the ribs are at this stage, allow them to cook for another 20-30 minutes.

4. Once your ribs are finished cooking, allow them to rest for about 15 minutes before cutting and serving.

ROASTED VEGETABLES

Brussels sprouts, carrots, and sweet potatoes with a light vinaigrette. Serves 2

INGREDIENTS:

1 pound Brussels sprouts, halved

2 carrots, diced

1 sweet potato, diced

3 tbsp Canola oil

1 tbsp + 1 tsp salt

2 tsp pepper

1 tbsp Dijon mustard

2 tbsp apple cider vinegar

1. Pre-heat oven or grill to 415 degrees.

2. Prepare vegetables by washing and cutting. Toss with 2 tbsp Canola oil, 1 tbsp salt, and 2 tsp pepper.

3. Line baking sheet with foil if using the oven. Place vegetables on sheet tray, or in a grill basket. If using a sheet pan, then flip each Brussels sprout so that the flat side is face down. Cover the vegetables with foil and place in the oven for 15 minutes. After 15 minutes, reduce temperature to 375, remove the foil and roast additional 20 minute. The vegetables should be tender and slightly browned. Otherwise, continue to roast the medley until they are fork tender then remove from oven.

4. Prepare vinaigrette by whisking Dijon mustard with apple cider vinegar. Then add 1 tbsp canola oil, 1 tsp salt, and a pinch of black pepper.

5. Allow vegetables to cool for 5 minutes and mix into a glass bowl. Add vinaigrette and gently stir until vegetables are evenly coated. Serve immediately or refrigerate and serve cold.

SPIKED CHERRY JUICE

Cherry soda with a kick! Makes 1 cocktail

INGREDIENTS:

1 ½ ounces whisky

1 orange wedge, squeezed

4 ounces of cherry soda (or substitute cherry juice)

Maraschino cherry for garnish

1. Chill a cocktail glass and fill with ice.

2. Measure whisky over ice. Squeeze orange juice into the glass.

3. Pour cherry soda into the glass and stir.

4. Garnish with cherry and enjoy!

Born in Wisconsin, I have always been inspired by travel and food (and a Webber grill). Time and money restrict traveling, but you can always experience culture through recipes and cooking. It is so rewarding to put time and effort into something that you can enjoy with your family and friends—especially before game time! I ditched the idea of my traditional college education and headed to the Windy City. With my culinary education and experience, I have found a nest with Whole Foods Market where we embrace our high quality standards and passion for food.

-Anna Hopkins

THE CLASSIC CHICAGO-STYLE HOT DOG

Submission by Baron W. Von Gottsacker
CEO of Bent Spoon Gelato, located in Sheboygan, Wisconsin

. . . .

Chicagoans are known for many things in the culinary world, but when it comes to the classic hot dog, things have to be just right. Any deviations from this, especially the addition of ketchup, would clearly not make this a Chicago Dog. Make sure your dogs are all beef and have a natural casing for that necessary "snap." Most Chicago Dogs are steamed or boiled, but cooking on the grill just adds that extra flavor that makes game day special.

. . . .

INGREDIENTS:

4 hot dog buns with poppy seeds

4 hot dogs (red hots, or Vienna Beef brand)

1 tomato, slice into half-moons

1 small white onion, diced

4 dill pickle spears

Yellow mustard

8 sport peppers

Sweet pickle relish (the brighter green, the better)

Celery salt

1. Pre-heat a grill

2. Slice an X onto the ends of each hot dog, about ½-inch deep. Place on the grill and cook about 4 minutes per side so that there is a good char on the hot dogs.

3. Spread your buns wide open, and add your hot dog to the middle.

4. On one side, add the mustard and tomato. On the other side add the relish and onion, wedging a pickle spear on top.

5. Finish off with the sport peppers and a dash of celery salt. Under no circumstances should ketchup be added as that would be considered sacrilegious in the Windy City.

ITALIAN MEATBALLS WITH MARINARA DIPPING SAUCE

By Paul Donaldson

....

This recipe takes a Chicago classic, the Italian sausage, off the grill and into a delicious Italian meatball served with a marinara dipping sauce. Serves 8-10

....

INGREDIENTS:

Meatballs:

1 ½ pounds ground Italian sausage

1 pound ground pork

2 tsp garlic powder

1 tsp white pepper

2 tsp dried parsley

1 ½ cups grated parmesan cheese

2 eggs

Vegetable oil (for frying)

Marinara sauce:

28 ounce can crushed tomatoes with sauce

2 tbsp olive oil

1 cup chopped onion

½ tsp dried basil

2 tsp garlic powder

1 tsp dried parsley

½ tsp dried oregano

½ tsp white pepper

Salt (to taste)

1. Make the marinara sauce. In a large saucepan, sauté the onion with olive oil over medium heat.

2. Add remaining ingredients to the saucepan and stir together.

3. Bring to a boil, then simmer for 15 minutes on low heat.

4. Serve in a dipping bowl.

5. Meanwhile, in a mixing bowl, beat the eggs together.

6. Add all of the additional meatball ingredients to the bowl, except for the vegetable oil.

7. Mix ingredients by hand and form into small 1-inch sized balls.

8. In a frying pan, add vegetable oil and heat over medium-high heat to about 350 degrees.

9. Fry meatballs until the center is cooked, 5-10 minutes, and then place on paper towel lined plate to soak up extra oil.

10. Transfer to a plate and serve with dipping sauce.

THE CHICAGO OLD FASHIONED

This classic Chicago cocktail is a great addition to any tailgating party.

Makes 1 cocktail

INGREDIENTS:

1 sugar cube (Demerara preferred)

3 dashes of orange bitters

3 ounces rye whiskey (preferred Koval Lion's Pride brand)

1 ½-inch orange slice

Orange peel (1-inch by ½-inch)

Ice

Bar napkin

1. Place bar napkin on top of a rocks glass, and place sugar cube in the center.

2. Soak the sugar cube with the three dashes of orange bitters

3. Roll the cube into the glass and muddle with the orange slice for about 30 seconds. Make sure to muddle only the fruit, and not the pith of the orange as it is bitter.

4. Add a few cubes of ice and half the whiskey. The ice and whiskey should be about level. Add a few more cubes of ice and the rest of the whiskey.

5. With the orange peel, rub the rim of the glass, then place peel in the drink.

CINCINNATI

CINCINNATI CHILI

Submission by Brandon Gee

If you've never tried it, you've still probably seen it on TV. Whenever there's a sporting event in Cincinnati, there seems to be a standard shot of people piling mounds of bright yellow cheese onto plates of chili and spaghetti. We don't care if you don't think it's chili, because well, it's not.

Its origin in Cincinnati dates back to the early 1920s when a pair of Macedonian immigrant brothers opened The Empress Chili Parlor downtown. They served a version of a Mediterranean stew, then toned down the spice level in order to make it palatable to the German immigrants that made up a large amount of the city's population at that time. Calling it 'chili' was really more of a marketing term, something easily recognizable to potential customers. To further Americanize their dish, they served their chili over hot dogs. It's believed the cheese became a part of the dish that way as well, because we Americans love piles of cheese.

Over the following decades, more neighborhood chili parlors popped up, each with their own spin on the dish that lost its Greek roots over time and became synonymous with its Midwestern home.

There are many variations of the recipe, and the much-debated (we have a lot of time on our hands) use of cocoa in the recipe is attributed to the Skyline chain, the most well-known restaurant. The biggest competitor's recipe, from Gold Star, is thinner and a bit spicier, tasting more like its southwestern cousin.

There's a bit of lingo that goes along with the dish:

A 3-way is just spaghetti, chili, and cheese. A 4-way adds kidney beans or chopped onions. A 5-way is both. Some local chili parlors offer 6 or 7-ways with the additions of garlic or jalapeños. Breath mints are a good idea for afterwards.

Continues on next page

INGREDIENTS:

2 onions, finely chopped

2 tsp olive oil

4 cloves garlic, minced

2 tbsp chili powder

1 tbsp paprika

1 tbsp cumin

1 tbsp coriander

1 tbsp salt

1 tsp pepper

1 ½ pounds ground beef

1 tsp oregano

1 tsp celery seed

3 tbsp cocoa powder

2 bay leaves

4 cups tomato sauce

2 cups chicken stock

2 tbsp apple cider vinegar

1 tbsp Worcestershire sauce

1 pound spaghetti

Cheddar cheese, finely shredded

1 can dark red kidney beans (optional)

Hot sauce (optional, for serving)

Oyster crackers (optional, for serving)

1. Sauté the onions in olive oil over medium heat until translucent, reserving some onions if you want to use as garnish.

2. Add garlic and sauté for 30 seconds. Add in chili powder, paprika, cumin, coriander, salt, and pepper. Stir until spices are fragrant, about 30 seconds.

3. Add ground beef and cook until meat is brown, draining excess fat from pan after meat is cooked through.

4. Add oregano, celery seed, bay leaves, and cocoa.

5. Add tomato sauce, chicken stock, vinegar, and Worcestershire. Bring to a boil then turn down heat to a simmer. Let mixture simmer on low heat for 25-30 minutes or until the chili is cooked down to a consistency akin to a sloppy joe.

6. Meanwhile, boil a pot of water and cook the spaghetti according to package directions.

7. When both are ready, line a plate with a healthy mound of spaghetti, pour chili over and top with cheddar cheese. Garnish as you wish.

Notes: This is a good alternative if serving this at a tailgate. Use plastic drinking cups (i.e. Solo brand, etc.), fill halfway with spaghetti, top with chili and cheese, etc. It's a much easier way to serve this way when you're tailgating.

The chili is also served as Cheese Coneys: The buns are traditionally lined with yellow mustard and raw onions, whatever style hot dog you choose, then topped with chili and a mound of cheddar cheese.

BUFFALO BENGAL DIP

By Conrad Klank

....

This meaty and spicy dip is easy to prepare at home, or you can grill the chicken and heat in a skillet on the grill when tailgating. Serves 6-8

....

INGREDIENTS:

2 8-ounce packages of cream cheese, softened to room temperature

¾ cup Frank's Red Hot Sauce, or your favorite brand

2 cups chicken, cooked and shredded

1 cup ranch salad dressing

1 ½ cup shredded cheddar cheese

1 green onion, chopped

Tortilla chips, for serving

1. Preheat oven or grill to 350 degrees.

2. In a medium bowl, stir together the cream cheese and hot sauce until blended together.

3. Mix in the ranch dressing, shredded chicken, and 1 cup of cheddar cheese into the mix.

4. Spoon evenly into a square baking dish. Top with remaining cheddar cheese.

5. Remove from oven or grill, top with chopped green onion, and serve with tortilla chips for dipping.

I am Stadium Journey's Ohio Correspondent. A Cincinnati native who somehow remains a Bengals fan despite their entire run through the 90s, some might say I'm a glutton for punishment. Writing for Stadium Journey in Ohio is interesting as I've gotten to experience every facet of major league sports and the wide range of stadiums of the state's many college football teams, from the mammoth Ohio Stadium to smaller settings like Nippert Stadium in Cincinnati and the Glass Bowl in Toledo.

-Brandon Gee

BEER FLOAT

This drink happens to highlight two ingredients that are pretty important to the Cincinnati area: beer and ice cream. Cincinnati's heritage is tied heavily to German immigrants and with that came a strong brewing tradition throughout the 1800s. Currently, the area is undergoing a renaissance with microbrewers like Mad Tree, 50 West, Mt. Carmel, Rivertowne, Rhinegeist, and Christian Moerlien along with other labels in Southwestern Ohio and Kentucky.

For this occasion, I actually went with a beer from Lexington, Kentucky's Alltech Brewery. Kentucky Bourbon Barrel Stout is a flavorful beer with 8.0% alcohol and a coffee flavor that stands up well to the ice cream. Really any higher alcohol stout (i.e. NOT Guinness) or a fruit-based lambic would work well.

As for the ice cream, I went with a vanilla from a local brand, Graeter's. All you need to know is Oprah loves it. Truthfully, it's a quality ice cream with a high butterfat content so it's much more rich than the standard grocery store options. Though I went with vanilla here, chocolate would work just as well.

Makes 1 cocktail (float)

INGREDIENTS:

Heavy stout beer

2 Scoops of vanilla or chocolate ice cream

1. Place a large scoop of ice cream in the pint glass.

2. Pour beer over the ice cream.

3. Top with another scoop of ice cream. Adding more beer if needed.

4. Drink, and wonder why you've never done this before.

CLEVELAND

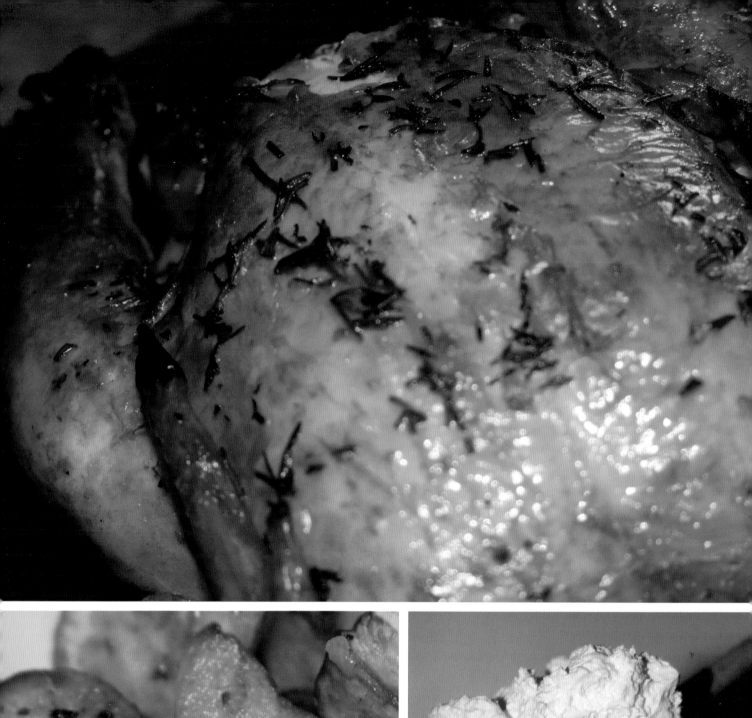

DAWG POUND CHICKEN

Submission by Joshua Guiher

A simple beer can chicken recipe using fresh herbs that will leave your guests howling.
Serves 8

INGREDIENTS:

2 whole chickens

2 cans of beer

½ cup vegetable shortening

¼ cup fresh rosemary, chopped

¼ cup fresh thyme, chopped

1. Pre-heat grill to 350 degrees.

2. Rinse chickens, then dry with paper towels. Coat generously with vegetable shortening.

3. Mix rosemary and thyme, then split into two piles. Coat each chicken with the herb mixture.

4. Open beer and slide opening of the chicken over the beer, keeping the can upright.

5. Wrap in foil and grill for about 90 minutes, or until chicken reaches an internal temperature of 165 degrees. Remove beer can and discard with care as contents will be very hot.

6. Carve chickens and serve.

A huge college football and NASCAR fan, I am attempting to see a game in every FBS stadium. To pay bills, I also own the Frasier Street Deli, a restaurant in State College, Pennsylvania, with my wife.

-Joshua Guiher

CLEVELAND'S BROWNED POTATOES

A hearty, tasty side dish to perfectly pair with the Dawg Pound Chicken. Serves 8

INGREDIENTS:

5 pounds redskin potatoes

½ cup (one stick) melted butter

2 tbsp fresh parsley

¼ cup minced garlic

½ cup chopped onion

1 tsp fresh rosemary, chopped

1 tsp fresh thyme, chopped

1. Preheat oven or grill to 350 degrees.

2. Wash potatoes and cut into bit-sized chunks of equal size.

3. Combine potatoes with remaining ingredients into a casserole pan and combine until evenly coated.

4. Bake potatoes until they are browned on the outside and fork tender, about 60 minutes.

HOT DAWG CIDER

Serves 8

INGREDIENTS:

2 ounces Tuaca vanilla-citrus liqueur

8 ounces apple cider

Cinnamon stick

Whipped cream

1. Warm apple cider in a small saucepan to desired temperature. Pour into a glass and combine with Tuaca.

2. Garnish with a cinnamon stick and whipped cream.

DALLAS

GRILLED CHICKEN TACOS WITH ROASTED PICO DE GALLO AND JALAPEÑO-CILANTRO CREAM SAUCE

Submission by Kathy Monteiro

. . . .

Dry-rubbed boneless, skinless chicken thighs grilled to perfection and topped with a fresh roasted corn pico de gallo and a creamy jalapeño-cilantro sauce. Serves 4

. . . .

INGREDIENTS:

2 pounds boneless, skinless chicken thighs

8 flour or corn tortillas, warmed

1 ½ tsp salt

1 tsp paprika

½ tsp black pepper

½ tsp cumin

½ tsp chili powder

½ tsp garlic powder

Roasted Corn Pico de Gallo:

1 ear of roasted corn, cut from cob

¾ cup Roma tomatoes, diced

¾ cup onion, diced

1 lime, juiced

Salt and pepper to taste

Jalapeño-Cilantro Cream Sauce:

1 cup onion, roughly chopped

1 jalapeño, roughly chopped with seeds removed depending on your desired level of spice

¾ cups cilantro

2 cloves garlic

16 ounces light sour cream

1 lime, zested and juiced

Salt and pepper to taste

1. Make the pico de gallo. Combine all ingredients in a small bowl, mixing well and refrigerating for an hour or more to allow flavors to meld.

2. Make jalapeño-cilantro cream sauce. Place onion, jalapeño, cilantro, and garlic in a food processor and pulse until smooth. Add remaining ingredients and pulse until you reach a sauce consistency. Refrigerate for at least an hour to allow flavors to meld.

3. Pre-heat grill or stovetop pan to medium (about 375 degrees).

4. In a small bowl, combine the salt, paprika, black pepper, chili powder, garlic powder, and ground cumin until thoroughly mixed.

5. Season the chicken liberally by rubbing on all sides.

6. Lightly oil the cooking surface and place chicken. Cook about 5-7 minutes per side, until completely cooked through.

7. Remove from heat to clean plate, cover and let rest for 5-10 minutes.

8. Slice thighs against the grain and assemble tacos with your choice of tortilla, layering the shell with chicken, pico de gallo, and sauce.

22 COWBOY JALAPEÑOS

Submission by Paul Donaldson

• •

In honor of one of the greatest running backs in the history of football, 22 Cowboy Jalapeños delivers a taste of Tex-Mex with the punch of a downhill runner. The jalapeños called for in this recipe may invoke fear just like the iconic Cowboy's star at midfield of AT&T Stadium. But fear not, the cream cheese filling cuts the heat and makes for a delicious appetizer. If tailgating, the jalapeño mixture can be made at home, and then you can cook from the tailgating party. Serves 4-6

• •

INGREDIENTS:

1 8-ounce package of cream cheese

1 pound hickory-smoked bacon, sliced

22 small to medium jalapeños

1. Remove bacon from packaging and place in the freezer for 10-15 to make it easier to cut.

2. Meanwhile, allow cream cheese to soften to room temperature on the kitchen counter.

3. Cut the tops off of the jalapeños and remove the seeds.

4. Boil jalapeños for about 15 minutes, or until fork tender.

5. Cut bacon into small pieces and cook until golden brown.

6. Put cream cheese in a bowl and pour bacon pieces over it (include grease from bacon for extra flavor). Mix well.

7. Stuff jalapeños with cream cheese mix, put on grill for 15-20 min to reheat and add smoky flavor for taste.

SHINER MARGARITA

Submission by Paul Donaldson

· ·

The Shiner Margarita is a quick blend of two great Texas flavors: margarita and Shiner Bock beer. Makes 2 cocktails

· ·

INGREDIENTS:

6 ounces frozen lime concentrate

6 ounces of water

3 ounces tequila

6 ounces of Shiner Bock beer (or substitute Mexican lager like Dos Equis)

Lime wedges for garnish

1. Combine frozen lime concentrate and water, stirring well until concentrate dissolves.

2. Add tequila and stir.

3. Add beer and stir.

4. Serve over ice. Garnish with a lime wedge.

DENVER

BEER-BATTERED TROUT TACOS

Submission by Rich Kurtzman

These beer-battered trout tacos will delight your senses. There's really nothing like fresh seafood prepared at home, especially when you live 1,000 miles from any ocean. But Colorado is known for our world-class trout fishing, and contains a multitude of lakes and rivers to find fresh trout any night of the week. Of course, if you don't live in Colorado – or somewhere near trout-fishing waters – you can always head down to the local grocer. One benefit of buying your trout instead of catching it yourself is the fact that the seafood butcher will clean and fillet the fish for you at no cost, making preparation that much quicker and easier. This method of preparing trout is quite easy indeed, and tastes so wonderful, you'll want to make it every time you catch one of those fantastic little fish. Serves 4

INGREDIENTS:

1 trout, skinless fillets

1 ½ cup flour

1 ½ tsp salt

1 tsp baking powder

1 tbsp olive oil

1 cup beer (recommend a Colorado porter, but substitute as needed)

1 tsp cayenne pepper

1 package flour tortillas

1 ripe avocado, sliced

Hot sauce (for serving, optional)

Safflower oil, for frying (substitute with vegetable oil if needed)

1. Combine 1 cup of flour with baking powder and salt. Make a well in the center of the mixture and add in the beer and olive oil, mixing thoroughly. If batter seems too thick, then add more beer.

2. Pour remaining ½ cup of flour on a plate and mix with cayenne pepper.

3. In a deep frying pan, warm oil to 350-375 degrees, using enough oil so that it is at least ½-inch deep.

4. Cut the trout into strips about 1-inch wide.

5. Dip strips into dry mixture, then dip into wet mixture and place in oil.

6. Cook fish for about 2-3 minutes, then flip. Trout is done when the color of batter is light brown and puffy.

7. Pull fish from oil and drain on paper towel-lined plate.

8. Serve with warm tortillas, avocado slices, and hot sauce.

MEXICAN-STYLE DENVER OMELET

This is a spicy version of the famed Denver Omelet, one that doesn't call for ham. It's quite tasty, and is bright and lively enough to wake up all of your senses. Perfect for the early kickoff time on a Sunday. Serves 2-4

INGREDIENTS:

2 tbsp olive oil

¼ white onion, chopped

2 cloves garlic, chopped

1 can chipotle peppers in adobo sauce (optional, leave it out if you don't want it spicy)

2 tbsp butter

3 eggs

Salt and pepper

3 ounces habanero cheddar cheese, cubed

1 avocado, sliced

1. In small sauté pan, heat the olive oil and cook onion and garlic with a sprinkle of salt and pepper for 3-5 minutes over medium heat.

2. If using the chipotles, add to the pan and cook for about 2-3 minutes. Remove pan from heat and allow ingredients to sit while preparing the eggs.

3. In a medium sauté pan, melt butter over medium heat. In a small bowl, whisk the eggs and pour into sauté pan.

4. Allow eggs to cook a bit, but not fully. When still wet, add sautéed veggies in a line across middle of eggs. Top with cheese.

5. Cover for 1-2 minutes. Gently fold over egg and place on a plate.

6. Cut into four triangles for individual servings and place sliced avocados on top and serve.

(Note: For less spicy appetizer, skip the chipotles and use a green or red bell pepper, diced. You can also add salsa on the side for those that can't live without spice!)

TEQUILA SUNSET

An end of the day, Latin-inspired cocktail, whose color is reminiscent of both the Colorado sunset and the Denver Broncos orange jerseys. Makes 1 cocktail

INGREDIENTS:

1 ounce tequila

Orange juice

½ ounce blackberry brandy

½ ounce grenadine

Ice

1. Fill a small glass with ice cubes.

2. Add tequila and blackberry brandy.

3. Fill glass with orange juice (avoid anything that says "made from concentrate").

4. Add a touch of grenadine.

5. Stir lightly and enjoy!

I am a Denver, Colorado native and currently reside in Fort Collins, about one hour north of the Centennial State's capital. I love spicy foods and creating my own edible concoctions. A Colorado State University alumnus, I am in the fifth year of my sportswriting career, acting as the Rocky Mountain Regional Correspondent for StadiumJourney.com, as well as a contributor for multiple other websites covering Colorado State athletics and the Denver Broncos. I am also trying my hand at becoming an author, penning my first book, and enjoy all types of outdoor activities such as fly fishing, camping, hiking, and grilling. Because Denver has a major Latin American influence, specifically many peoples with Mexican heritage, my dishes are Mexican-themed. Enjoy and watch out for the spice if that's not your fancy!

-Rich Kurtzman

DETROIT

KIELBASA STEW

Submission by Paul Swaney

....

Kielbasas are a classic Polish smoked sausage which is wonderful for tailgating because they don't require a lot of cooking. Just throw them on the grill to warm them up and you're ready to go. They also make a great soup, which is perfect on a cold day when you're tailgating. Or make your life really easy and make this a day in advance, and just place the pot on the grill when you get to the game. Either way, this spicy stew will be a delicious way to warm you up. With a large Polish population, this is the right sausage for tailgating in Detroit. Bring coffee mugs to serve if tailgating to make it easier to eat. Serves 8-10

....

INGREDIENTS:

1 tbsp olive oil

1 pound kielbasa, sliced

½ large onion, chopped (about 1 cup)

1 green pepper, chopped (about 1 cup)

6 small carrots, chopped (about 1 cup)

4 cloves garlic, chopped

1 can great northern or cannellini beans, drained and rinsed

2 cups chicken broth

1 tsp paprika

1 tsp dried parsley

½ tsp crushed red pepper flakes (optional)

Salt and pepper

1. Heat olive oil in a soup pot or Dutch oven over medium heat.

2. Add kielbasa and carrots and cook until sausage begins to brown, about 5 minutes.

3. Add onions and green pepper and cook until onions begin to soften, about 5 minutes.

4. Add garlic and cook 1 additional minute.

5. Add beans and chicken stock and bring to a boil.

6. Reduce heat to low and add paprika, dried parsley, red pepper flakes, and salt and pepper to taste.

GRILLED SQUID SALAD

While octopus is more associated with Detroit sports, we substitute squid here as it is easier to prepare and usually easier to find in stores. When shopping, you may want to call ahead, or check with your local fish monger. If you decide to use octopus, then the preparation will be similar, except that you will want to cook the octopus in the marinade for about 30 minutes over medium heat, using water to cover if necessary. Follow the rest of the instructions as is. Serves 6

INGREDIENTS:

Squid and marinade:

1 ½ pounds cleaned squid, bodies only

½ cup diced white onion

4 cloves crushed garlic

Top of one fennel bulb, diced (about ½ cup)

Juice of one large lemon

1 cup chianti (or other dry Mediterranean wine)

¼ cup olive oil

1 tsp dried oregano

1 bay leaf

Pinch of salt and pepper

Salad:

1 bulb of fennel sliced very thinly

1 tomato diced

3 ounces feta cheese, diced

12-16 Kalamata olives, coarsely chopped

1-2 sprigs of mint, sliced

Fennel fronds for garnish

Dill (optional for garnish)

Dressing:

Juice of one lemon

1 tsp chianti

3 tsp red wine vinegar

¼ cup of good olive oil

Pinch of salt and pepper

1 clove minced garlic (optional)

1. If using frozen squid, thaw overnight in the refrigerator or by running under cold water for about an hour in a colander in the sink. When ready, rinse and then dry thoroughly.

2. Place whole squid in a gallon size plastic bag, or in a bowl. Add the other ingredients of the marinade and place in refrigerator for at least 30 minutes. If tailgating, place in your cooler and allow to marinate until you get to the game.

3. Combine the salad ingredients, except mint, dill, and fennel fronds, in a gallon size plastic bag, and place in refrigerator, or cooler if tailgating.

4. Combine salad dressing ingredients in a small plastic container and shake well to incorporate. Place in refrigerator, or cooler if tailgating.

5. Pre-heat grill until hot.

6. Place squid on grill and cook about 2 minutes per side. Remove from grill, and once cool enough to handle, cut squid into bite-sized rings.

7. Combine squid with salad ingredients and then pour over dressing. Close container and shake to incorporate. Place salad in a bowl and top with mint, dill, and fennel fronds.

HONOLULU BLUE LIONHEART

Inspired by the team's official colors and nickname, as well as my home town of Traverse City, MI (The Cherry Capital of the World), this tropical drink is sweet, strong, and satisfying. Makes 1 cocktail

INGREDIENTS:

⅓ cup pineapple juice

⅓ cup white rum

⅓ cup blue curacao liqueur

4 frozen black sweet cherries

1. Use the cherries as ice cubes. Combine the liquid ingredients and pour over cherries. You'll be left with four cherries representing the four chambers of a lion's heart. If the color of the drink doesn't mimic the uniforms of the Lions enough, then just add more blue curacao.

GREEN BAY

THE PERFECT WISCONSIN BRAT

Submission by Baron W. Von Gottsacker

If there is one thing that Wisconsin is known for, it's cheese. But if there are two things, then that second item would be the bratwurst. This recipe shows you how to prepare the perfect brat for your tailgating or home viewing party. Serves 4-6

INGREDIENTS:

4-6 bratwursts

4-6 rolls

Pickles, ketchup, brown mustard, and
onion as condiments

1. Pack the sausages into a vacuum bag (4 to 6 sausages per bag) and seal. If your sausages came vacuum packed you can use that bag as well.

2. Poach the sausages at 140 degrees for 2-3 hours.

3. There are multiple ways to achieve this water temperature:

4. You can use an immersion circulator with a water bath to achieve this temperature. Or you can place a pot of water on the stove and heat until the desired temp is achieved. When dealing with the pot on stove method, remember that once you add the sausages the water temperature will drop. Increase the heat for a bit to compensate. You will have to keep an eye on the temperature until it stabilizes. Half an hour before the sausages are done poaching, start the fire on the charcoal grill.

5. Once cooked, pull from the package and sear on the hot charcoal grill to crisp up the skin.

6. In Wisconsin we serve two brats on a hard roll, with the works (pickle, ketchup, brown mustard, and onion). No yellow mustard!

GREEN AND GOLD SALAD

This festive and delicious salad will also ensure you have plenty of extra room for that second bratwurst. We use yellow raspberries, but other yellow fruits could be used, including golden delicious apples, nectarines, or golden plums. Serves 4

INGREDIENTS:

8 ounces arugula (preferably organic)

8 ounces baby spinach (preferably organic)

4 ounces coat cheese (chèvre)

Candied walnuts

1 pound yellow raspberries (or red if you can't find yellow)

FOR THE DRESSING:

½ cup blood orange juice

1 small shallot, peeled and chopped

2 tbsp balsamic vinegar

2 tbsp sugar

Salt to taste

2 tbsp olive oil

1. Make the dressing. Puree shallot in blender with blood orange juice, sugar, and balsamic vinegar.

2. Turn blender on high and slowly drizzle olive oil in, until it's emulsified. Season to taste.

3. Toss salad greens with enough dressing to coat leaves.

4. Divide salad into 4 bowls, top with yellow raspberries, crumbled goat cheese, and candied walnuts.

BEST YERLO OLD FASHIONED

Submission by Po Lo

....

For many years I had the vision of creating a product that would reflect my passion for sharing the Hmong People's rich heritage. After years of perfecting and distilling traditional Hmong rice spirits with my mother and attending distilling seminars and workshops, I used my dedication and knowledge to start my own artisan distillery. Being a business owner for over 8 years, I am energized to create a long-lasting product and establishment that the public will enjoy in Yerlo: Hmong Rice Spirits and Whiskey. Makes 1 cocktail

....

INGREDIENTS:

1 sugar cube

1 orange, zested and then sliced

2 ½ ounces Yerlo X (or any sweet bourbon/whiskey)

2 maraschino cherries

Angostura bitters

Water

Ice cubes

1. Put sugar cube in a glass and drop in 5-6 dashes of bitters. Add the juice from one maraschino cherry and three dashes of water. Muddle sugar cube until it is almost dissolved. Add orange zest and gently muddle once.

2. Add two ice cubes and stir three times. Add in 1 ounce of Yerlo X, and stir two more times. Repeat by adding two ice cubes and 1 ounce of Yerlo X, and stir two times. Add another ice cube and ½ ounce of Yerlo X, and stir twice.

3. Add a cherry and serve.

HOUSTON

CHORIZO TACOS WITH PICKLED CUCUMBER-RADISH SALAD

Submission by Kathy Monteiro

....

Rich Mexican Chorizo sausage paired with a crisp, refreshing pickled cucumber-radish salad and salty cotija cheese. All wrapped up in your favorite flour or corn tortilla. Serves 4

....

INGREDIENTS:

1 package Johnsonville chorizo sausage links

1 cup grated cotija cheese

8 flour or corn tortillas, warmed

PICKLED CUCUMBER-RADISH SALAD:

1 cup English cucumbers, sliced

1 cup radishes, sliced

2 tbsp red wine vinegar

2 tbsp olive oil

Salt and pepper to taste

1. Make the salad a few hours before serving or overnight. Mix all salad ingredients in a glass or plastic container and place in the refrigerator until ready to serve.

2. Pre-heat grill or stovetop pan to about 375 degrees over medium heat.

3. Place chorizo links on cooking surface (if using a pan, spray with cooking spray or a little oil before adding links), turning links until completely cooked (15-20 minutes).

4. Transfer the links to a platter, cover and let rest for 5-10 minutes.

5. Slice sausages diagonally into ¼-inch slices.

6. Assemble tacos with sausage on tortillas and top with cotija cheese and salad.

SIMPLY DELICIOUS GUACAMOLE

The simplest of Tex-Mex appetizers. Fresh, delicious and oh so easy to make! Makes about 2 cups

INGREDIENTS:

3 cloves garlic

¼ cup red onion, finely chopped

1 Roma tomato, finely diced

2 large ripe Haas avocadoes

½ lemon, juiced

½ jalapeño, finely chopped (optional)

Salt and pepper to taste

1. Combine all ingredients and mix to desired consistency.

2. Serve with tortilla chips and favorite vegetables. To make this appetizer extra special, cut fresh corn tortillas using a Texas shaped cutter and deep fry until golden brown.

THE "GRAHAM" MARGARITA

A zingy take on a traditional Tex-Mex favorite. A simple margarita recipe that is kicked up with muddled jalapeño and cilantro. Makes 4 cocktails

INGREDIENTS:

4 ounces tequila

4 ounces Cointreau

4 ounces lime juice

½ jalapeño, seeds removed

Handful of cilantro stems and leaves, more for garnish if desired

Sprite

1. In a cocktail shaker, muddle the jalapeño and cilantro to release their natural oils and juices.

2. Add tequila, Cointreau, lime juice, and healthy splash of Sprite. Shake gently to blend.

3. Pour mixture into a margarita glass filled with ice and a salted or sugared rim (if desired), straining muddled jalapeño and cilantro.

4. Garnish with a sprig of cilantro and enjoy!

INDIANAPOLIS

TURDUCKEN CORDON BLUE BURGER

Submission by Scott Kammerer

....

One of the greatest spectacles in food. The Turducken Cordon Bleu Burger is one patty comprised of layers of ground turkey and ground chicken sandwiching a slice of Maple Leaf Farms duck breast wrapped in duck bacon! Top that with thin slices of smoked ham and Swiss cheese and a generous amount of sweet corn aioli; how could this burger get any better? Serves 4

....

INGREDIENTS:

Chicken patty:

½ pound ground chicken, dark meat preferred

1 tsp fresh garlic

1 tsp Cajun seasoning

½ tsp Old Bay seasoning

Pinch of kosher salt

Turkey patty:

½ pound ground turkey

1 tsp poultry seasoning

Pinch of kosher salt

Sweet corn aioli:

1 cup mayonnaise

1 lemon, zested and juiced

4 cloves garlic, minced

1 cup fresh grilled or frozen sweet corn

Remaining ingredients:

4-6 ounce duck breast (from Maple Leaf Farms if possible)

8 slices duck bacon (substitute regular bacon if you can't find duck bacon)

8 slices smoked ham (about 6 ounces)

4 slices Swiss cheese

4 hamburger buns (remember the better the bun, the better the burger so don't skimp)

Sliced tomatoes and lettuce if desired

1. Mix the ground chicken, garlic, Cajun seasoning, seafood spice, and salt together and form 4 equal 4 to 5-inch patties. You will want them thin. Set aside on a sheet of parchment.

2. Mix the ground turkey, poultry seasoning, and salt together and form 4 equally thin 4 to 5-inch patties.

3. Quarter duck breast by slicing first the thickness and then the length to get four equal slices about ⅜-inch thick.

Continues on next page

4. Wrap duck breast slices in duck bacon and sear over medium heat. This will speed up the grill time and make a juicier burger.

5. Place the seared duck breast (and pan drippings) on top of the chicken patty and top with the turkey patty, and press the edges to seal into one patty with the duck in the center. Continue with the remaining patties.

6. Place on grill; approximately 5-6 minutes on each side. Be sure the center reaches 160 degrees.

7. Make the aioli. Place mayo, zest, lemon juice, garlic, and corn into a food processor and pulse a few times until fairly smooth.

8. Place buns on the grill when the burgers are almost finished and toast.

9. Coat both halves of the bun with the aioli. Place the burger on the bottom bun, add cheese and warmed ham. Top with lettuce and tomato.

I have been the Executive Chef and Culinary Director at Parkview Field in Fort Wayne, Indiana, since its inaugural season in 2009. Thanks to a five-star food and beverage rating, the home of the Fort Wayne TinCaps — Class-A affiliate San Diego Padres — has been named the No. 1 ballpark in all of Minor League Baseball by Stadium Journey Magazine in 2011 and 2012. My kitchen at Parkview Field serves more than 400,000 meals per year across a 70-game baseball schedule and catering for 450-plus special events. I have implemented healthy methods of cooking and working with fresh produce, and have also led Parkview Field to a No. 4 ranking in PETA's 2013 poll of Top 10 Vegetarian-Friendly Minor League Ballparks.

Born and raised in Fort Wayne, I developed a passion for the culinary industry and food at an early age. With a unique style, flair, and knowledge base shaped by working under influential leaders of the Fort Wayne culinary profession, I have become a principal performer in the Summit City's culinary community. Though opportunities have existed elsewhere, I have never strayed far from home in the Hoosier State, where I have been able to enjoy my career and raise four children with my wife.

When not in the kitchen at Parkview Field, I share my culinary passion and talents with younger chefs and local charities in Fort Wayne. I volunteer with the hospitality program at Indiana University-Purdue University Fort Wayne, while also preparing meals for Vincent Village, an organization that cares for the homeless.

-Scott Kammerer

BBQ FOOTBALLS

Very moist and flavorful BBQ Meatballs in the shape of footballs. Serves 4

INGREDIENTS:

1 pound ground beef

¼ pound ground pork (or substitute chicken or turkey)

1 egg

¼ cup shredded asiago cheese

1 tbsp milk

1 tbsp oregano

1 tbsp corn starch

1 tbsp mustard

1 tsp fresh parsley, chopped

1 clove garlic, chopped

1 tsp celery seed

1 tsp onion powder

1 quart of your favorite BBQ sauce

1. Mix all ingredients in a large mixing bowl.

2. Roll into 16 equally sized balls, about 1 ¼ ounces each, then roll into a football shape.

3. Place in an oven at 325 degrees for 20 minutes.

4. Meanwhile, heat BBQ sauce in a saucepan.

5. Remove meatballs from the oven and cover with BBQ sauce and serve.

HORSEPOWER!

A delightful crisp cocktail with a kick! Makes 4 cocktails

INGREDIENTS:

24 ounces of 7up

4 ounces of vodka, chilled

2 ounces tequila

4 ounces blue curacao

16 ounces Rockstar Energy drink

4 pieces of lemon peel for garnish

1. Fill glasses with ice.

2. Pour 4 ounces of Rockstar Energy drink into each glass.

3. Add 1 ounce of vodka, 1 ounce of blue curacao, and ½ ounce tequila to each glass.

4. Top with 7up, garnish with the lemon peel and serve.

JACKSONVILLE

BLACKENED MAHI MAHI SANDWICH WITH COCONUT KEY LIME SLAW

Submission by Christopher Crump

....

This sandwich brings big tropical flavors to your party using local mahi mahi, coconut, and the tartness of Key limes. Serves 8

....

INGREDIENTS:

8 5-ounce fillets of mahi mahi (or grouper as substitute)

8 Kaiser rolls, sliced

2 cups red cabbage, chopped

2 cups green cabbage, chopped

1 can light coconut milk

1 cup fresh mango, diced

1 orange, zested

¼ cup Greek yogurt

1 tbsp honey

1 jalapeño, diced

4 Key limes, juiced

1 cup vegetable oil

1 tbsp cayenne pepper

1 cup blackening seasoning (Cajun seasoning)

Salt and pepper

1. Combine coconut milk, honey, yogurt, lime juice, orange zest, salt, and pepper and whisk together. Add mango, cabbage, jalapeño, and season to taste. Toss together and refrigerate until serving (can be made the day before).

2. Pre-heat grill to medium high-heat.

3. Lightly brush fish with vegetable oil, then coat both sides with blackening seasoning, a pinch of cayenne, and salt and pepper. Place on grill for 4 minutes or until cooked half-way through, then turn. Continue to cook until cooked all the way through.

4. Remove from grill. Place fresh rolls on grill for 1 minute or until golden brown.

5. Place fish on toasted roll and top with coconut slaw and serve.

SUNSHINE PEEL AND EAT SHRIMP WITH PINEAPPLE AND SERRANO COCKTAIL SAUCE

My version of this coastal favorite combines the heat of Serrano peppers with the sweetness of golden pineapple. Serves 10-12

INGREDIENTS:

2 pounds 16-20 count Gulf shrimp, deveined

2 tbsp Old Bay seasoning

3 lemons, halved

¼ cup whole peppercorns

2 bay leaves

10 cloves garlic, crushed

¼ cup kosher sea salt

2 tbsp vegetable oil

1 20-ounce can crushed pineapple with juices

½ Serrano pepper, seeded and chopped

1 cup water

3 limes, juiced

1 shallot, diced

3 ounces coconut rum

2 quarts ice

Salt and pepper

Lemon and lime wedges for garnish

1. Make the cocktail sauce. Heat vegetable oil in saucepan over medium heat, add shallots and Serrano and cook for 3 minutes or until caramelization begins to occur.

2. Add lime juice, pineapple, rum, and water. Let the mixture reduce on medium heat for 20-30 minutes or until a salsa-like consistency is achieved.

3. Remove from heat and pour into blender or food processor. Puree for 1 minute. Pour sauce into serving dish and refrigerate at least 2 hours before serving.

4. Combine 4 quarts water and 2 quarts ice in large container and set aside.

5. Meanwhile, bring 4 quarts of water to a boil with Old Bay seasoning, lemons, peppercorns, garlic, and salt. Allow to boil for about 5 minutes, then add shrimp. Continue to boil for 5 minutes longer.

6. Remove shrimp quickly and place in the ice water bath to stop the cooking process. Let shrimp cool in ice bath for about 10 minutes.

7. After chilled, rinse under cold water and let drain for 10 minutes. After shrimp are dry, chill in fridge up to 24 hours before serving. Place shrimp and cocktail sauce on large platter. Garnish with lemon and lime wedges.

CLASSIC HURRICANE

....

This classic rum cocktail that originated in New Orleans has made landfall in North Florida. Makes 1 cocktail

....

INGREDIENTS:

2 ounces light rum

2 ounces dark rum

2 ounces passion fruit juice

1 ounce orange juice

Juice of ½ lime

1 tbsp grenadine

1 tbsp simple syrup

1. Fill a cocktail glass with ice and squeeze lime juice over ice.

2. Combine remaining ingredients in a cocktail shaker and shake vigorously. Pour over ice and serve.

KANSAS CITY

BBQ PULLED PORK SANDWICH

Submission by Anna Hopkins

. . . .

Delicious pork sandwiched between a pretzel roll and sweet, spicy BBQ sauce!
Makes 4 sandwiches

. . . .

INGREDIENTS:

1 ½ pounds bone-in pork shoulder

½ cup dry rub (see recipe below)

1 package smoking chips

Charcoal

1 clove garlic

1 ⅓ cups ketchup

½ cup apple cider vinegar

3 tbsp brown sugar

10 dashes Worcestershire sauce

1 tbsp molasses

1 tsp black pepper

½ tsp cayenne pepper

½ tsp salt

4 pretzel rolls

Dry rub:

¼ cup salt

⅓ cup dark brown sugar

3 tbsp + 1 tsp chili powder

1 tbsp cayenne pepper

2 tbsp paprika

½ tsp allspice

1 tbsp dried oregano

1 tbsp + 1 tsp black pepper

1 tbsp garlic salt

1 tbsp cumin

1. Combine ingredients for dry rub together and mix thoroughly.

2. Rub dry rub on pork shoulder, and refrigerate for 12 hours or more.

3. Prepare your home smoker (refer to page 31 for instructions).

4. Smoke pork on opposite side of charcoal. Allow to smoke for 2-3 hours. Monitor temperature every 30 minutes to maintain a temperature of 225 degrees. Once pork is tender, remove from grill.

5. Allow pork to rest for 20 minutes and pull apart for your sandwiches.

6. While pork is cooking, prepare BBQ sauce. Heat a saucepot with the ketchup, vinegar, Worcestershire sauce, sugar, pepper, cayenne, and salt. Whisk thoroughly until combined and simmer for 20 minutes.

7. To assemble sandwiches, warm pretzel buns and slice in half.

8. Pile pork on top and slather with BBQ sauce.

RED SLAW

Crunchy cabbage with a sweet BBQ sauce. Serves 4

INGREDIENTS:

½ head red cabbage, thinly chopped

½ head green cabbage, thinly chopped

2 carrots, shredded

1 cup sweet and spicy BBQ sauce

1. Mix together cabbage and carrots.

2. Add chilled BBQ sauce to cabbage and mix thoroughly. Serve on the side of your sandwiches or right on top!

MULE CIDER ON ICE

Sweet bourbon with a tart apple flavor. Makes 1 cocktail

INGREDIENTS:

1 ounce bourbon

1 ounce Apple Jack

3 ounces apple cider

2 apple wedges, diced

1 tsp lemon juice

1 tsp lemon zest

1. Mix together cabbage and carrots.

2. Pour bourbon, Apple Jack, and apple cider in a rocks glass with ice. Add diced apples, lemon juice, and lemon zest. Stir and serve!

MIAMI

CUBAN-SPICED FLAT IRON STEAK WITH SALSA VERDE

Submission by Paul Swaney

....

I love flat iron steak cooked to a perfect medium rare, then sliced thin. It makes for a great game day presentation, especially when served with this bright salsa verde. This dish is easy to prepare, impressive to present, and absolutely delicious. Serves 4-6

....

INGREDIENTS:

2 pounds flat iron steaks (about 2 steaks)

Cumin, salt, and pepper

Salsa Verde:

4 green onions, chopped

1 handful cilantro

1 jalapeño (optional), seeded and chopped

2 cloves garlic

¼ cup olive oil

2 tbsp lime juice (about one lime)

¼ tsp pepper

¼ tsp salt

1. Remove steaks from refrigerator. Season the steaks generously with cumin, salt, and pepper, and allow to come to room temperature for about 30-40 minutes.

2. Light a grill at warm to medium, or about 450 degrees when covered. Brush grill with some olive oil.

3. Meanwhile, in a food processor, combine all ingredients and run until you have a sauce-like consistency. If you are tailgating, you can make the salsa verde ahead of time. If you prepare at the game, then just cut up ingredients as small as possible for a chunkier topping to your steaks.

4. Place steaks on the grill and cook for 7 minutes, rotating 45 degrees halfway through to achieve beautiful crisscross grill marks. Flip and cook for an additional 6 minutes.

5. Remove steaks from the grill and allow to rest for 5-10 minutes. Slice steaks against the grain into thin strips and place on a warmed serving platter. Top with salsa verde and serve.

BLACK BEAN SALSA

....

Another easy to make, Cuban-inspired dish. This salsa can also be served with the flat iron steak above, or with tortilla chips as a flavorful snack.

....

INGREDIENTS:

1 can black beans, drained and rinsed

2 small Roma tomatoes, chopped

2 cloves garlic, chopped

¼ cup olive oil

1 tbsp lime juice (about ½ a lime)

1 tsp cumin

¼ tsp salt

¼ tsp pepper

¼ tsp red pepper flakes, or cayenne pepper (optional)

1 green onion, chopped for garnish

Tortilla chips for serving

1. Combine all of the ingredients in a food processor and blend until desired consistency. Taste and adjust seasonings as necessary. Pulse again.

2. Pour into a bowl. Top with green onions. Serve with tortilla chips.

THE BLUE DOLPHIN

....

Fruity and sweet, this tropical cocktail makes you feel like you're in South Florida. Makes 1 cocktail

....

INGREDIENTS:

1 orange, zested

1 tsp sugar

1 slice of orange

Ice

2 ounces blue curacao

1 ounce white rum

½ ounce Midori

7up

1. Combine the orange zest and sugar on a small plate, mixing well so that the sugar looks orange.

2. Rub the slice of orange along the rim of a tumbler glass, then dip in the orange sugar mixture until the rim is covered.

3. Fill the tumbler with ice.

4. Add blue curacao, white rum, and Midori. Stir.

5. Top with 7up and garnish with the orange slice.

MINNESOTA

WALLEYE AND WILD RICE CHOWDER

Submission by Paul Swaney

....

The state grain of Minnesota (wild rice) meets one of the state's most prevalent fish in this hearty chowder. Consider making this at home and bringing it to the tailgating and just heating it on the grill. Coffee mugs are great serving devices for soup when tailgating. Serves 6

....

INGREDIENTS:

½ pound of skinless walleye fillet (substitute other whitefish if needed)

½ cup uncooked wild rice

½ cup white onion, diced

½ cup celery, sliced

1 cup red potato, diced

3 cloves garlic, minced

2 tbsp butter

3 sprigs thyme

2 tsp Old Bay seasoning

2 cups vegetable or fish stock

2 cups half and half

1 tbsp lemon juice

5 slices of bacon, cooked and diced

Fresh parsley and green onion for garnish

1. Prepare rice according to package instructions.

2. Cook bacon and set aside.

3. Meanwhile, melt the butter in a Dutch oven or soup pot over medium heat. Add in onions and celery and cook for 3 minutes. Add in garlic and cook for 2 additional minutes.

4. Add stock, potatoes, thyme, lemon juice, and Old Bay seasoning. Bring to a boil, lower to a simmer, and cook covered for 15 minutes.

5. Add in fish and bacon. Bring back to a boil, then simmer again for 5 minutes.

6. Add in rice and cream, and simmer for 5 more minutes before serving. Add in salt and pepper to taste.

7. Garnish with parsley and green onions as desired.

BLUEBERRY MUFFIN BREAD

Minnesota is one of the only states with an official state muffin. This recipe turns the muffin into a loaf of bread, which is a great way to start your football Sunday. Plus those blueberries look purple when baked. Make this at home and bring to the tailgate or serve with breakfast on Vikings game days. Top slices with cream cheese and honey. Makes 1 loaf, about 10 servings

INGREDIENTS:

2 cups flour

1 ½ tsp baking powder

½ tsp salt

2 cups fresh blueberries

1 lemon, zested

1 cup sugar

1 stick of butter, at room temperature

2 eggs

½ cup vanilla yogurt

Room temperature cream cheese and honey for serving

1. Preheat oven to 350 degrees. Spray bread pan with cooking spray.

2. In a large bowl, combine the flour, baking powder, and salt. Add in the whole blueberries and lemon zest and toss together gently so as not to break the berries.

3. In a separate bowl, cream together the butter and sugar. Add the eggs and slowly beat into the mixture. Add the yogurt and mix again.

4. Add in the dry ingredients and mix until you have a bread batter, taking care not to break the berries.

5. Use a rubber spatula and spoon mixture into bread pan. Bake for one hour until lightly browned. Let cool for about 10 minutes, then transfer to a plate for slicing and serving.

6. If desired, spread cream cheese and drizzle honey on bread slices

PURPLE PEOPLE EATER PUNCH

A variation on a French Martini, this cocktail is strong, delicious, and will make you feel like a Viking. Makes 1 cocktail

INGREDIENTS:

⅓ cup vodka

¼ cup raspberry liqueur

¼ cup pineapple juice

Ice

1. Fill a cocktail shaker with ice.

2. Add ingredients and shake well.

3. Pour into a chilled martini glass or tumbler and serve.

NEW ENGLAND

CLASSIC LOBSTER ROLL

Submission by Kristen Merrill

....

You can't do much better for New England eating than a classic lobster roll. Adding lemon zest and a touch of tarragon brightens the classic flavor of this favorite dish. Lining the buns with lettuce keeps the bread from becoming soggy if not serving immediately. Serves 4

....

INGREDIENTS:

4 New England split-top buns

3 "chicken" lobsters, steamed and disassembled, meat only

2 tbsp butter, softened

4 tbsp mayonnaise

3 tsp fresh tarragon, finely chopped

1 ½ tsp lemon zest

4 leaves Boston lettuce, washed and thoroughly dried

Salt and pepper to taste

Dash of smoked paprika

1. Spread outside of buns with butter.

2. Toast buns on a grill or in a pan. Remove from heat when golden brown.

3. Combine lobster meat with mayonnaise, tarragon, lemon zest, and a pinch of salt and pepper.

4. Line each bun with a leaf of Boston lettuce.

5. Divide lobster meat mixture between four rolls.

6. Sprinkle smoked paprika on top of each roll before serving.

A born and bred New Englander, Kristen grew up cheering passionately for all of Boston's teams. Marrying a New York fan just made her cheer harder. In graduate school at Boston University, Kristen studied New England food traditions and loved creating regional specialties, especially for tailgating!

BOSTON BAKED BEANS WITH VERMONT MAPLE SYRUP AND SAUSAGE

Vermont maple syrup and sausage create a hearty appetizer with New England written all over it. Serve with cornbread for a true New England feel. You can also use dried beans for this recipe, but you will need to soak them 24 hours ahead of time and soften them by boiling prior to baking. Make your life easier and use the canned beans. Serves 6-8

INGREDIENTS:

4 slices bacon, diced

1 yellow onion, diced

2 cloves garlic, minced

1 yellow bell pepper, seeded and diced

½ green bell pepper, seeded and diced

2 15-ounce cans navy beans, drained and rinsed

2 15-ounce cans pinto beans, drained and rinsed

4 links smoked kielbasa, sliced

½ cup Vermont maple syrup

4 tbsp tomato paste

2 tsp dried ground mustard

½ cup molasses

½ cup ketchup

¼ cup apple cider vinegar

2 tbsp brown sugar

1. Preheat oven or grill to 350 degrees.

2. In a large pot over medium-high heat, sauté bacon until fat is rendered and bacon is slightly crispy.

3. Remove bacon from pot with a slotted spoon and set aside.

4. Sauté onions, garlic, and peppers in bacon fat in pot until translucent and fragrant but not browned, about five minutes.

5. Add beans, kielbasa, and cooked bacon to pot with vegetables. Stir to combine.

6. In a large bowl, whisk together maple syrup, tomato paste, mustard, molasses, ketchup, vinegar, and brown sugar.

7. Add maple syrup mixture to pot of beans, stir to combine.

8. Transfer bean mixture to oven-safe baking dish or skillet and bake at 350 degrees for 1 to 1 ½ hours, until browned and bubbly. Serve with bread or cornbread.

CRANBERRY MAPLE RUM MASH

Boston has a long and storied history with rum (just ask Bostonians about the Great Molasses Flood of 1919). Combining rum with regional specialties like cranberries and maple syrup results in a cocktail that tastes like autumn in New England. Perfect on a cold game day. Makes 2 cocktails

INGREDIENTS:

6 ounces light rum (Bully Boy is a Boston local brand that works great for this recipe)

1 ounce Vermont maple syrup

½ cup plus ¼ cup fresh cranberries

½ cup sugar

½ water

1. Create a cranberry simple syrup by combining sugar, water, and ½ cup cranberries in a small saucepan until the sugar dissolves and cranberries start to burst. Muddle mixture to ensure that all berries are smashed.

2. Remove simple syrup from the heat and strain through a fine mesh strainer, removing all berry pulp and seeds. You should be left with a reddish sugar syrup.

3. In a cocktail shaker, add ice and combine rum with simple syrup and maple syrup. Shake vigorously.

4. Serve in tall cocktail glasses over ice. Garnish with remaining fresh cranberries.

NEW ORLEANS

RED BEANS AND RICE WITH ANDOUILLE SAUSAGE

Submission by Paul Donaldson

While this dish is foreign to most outside of Cajun country, I grew up eating red beans and rice as a weekly staple meal. Whether served up in front of the television while watching the game or at the tailgate, this dish is classically New Orleans. Serves 8

INGREDIENTS:

8 cups of water

1 package dried red kidney beans

1 package of Andouille sausage, thinly sliced

1 12-ounce package of Pictsweet seasoning blend (or other frozen vegetable mix)

1 tbsp garlic powder

1 tbsp seasoning salt

1 tbsp dried parsley flakes

1 tbsp salt

3-4 shakes of Louisiana hot sauce or Tabasco sauce

1. Place all ingredients except sausage in crock pot on high heat.

2. Cook for 6 hours, covered. Check water level, if the beans need more water or the consistency is too pasty, then add water to compensate.

3. Sautee sliced Andouille sausage in a pan until browned. Add sausage and drippings to crockpot; stir and cook 2 additional hours.

4. Serve over rice.

Born and raised in Louisiana, I have two loves in life: football and food. Whether it's professional or college football, I am in the stands and looking for sports grub to eat. I have been with the Stadium Journey team since 2012.

-Paul Donaldson

FRIED PICKLES WITH REMOULADE SAUCE

Serves 8

INGREDIENTS:

1 jar of whole pickles

2 cups flour

2 cups panko bread crumbs

4 tbsp seasoning salt (Tony Chachere's preferred)

1 egg

2 cups whole milk

Vegetable oil (for frying)

Remoulade Sauce:

1 ¼ cups mayonnaise

5 ounces creole mustard

¼ cup ketchup

2 tsp Tabasco

2 tsp creamed horseradish sauce

1 tsp Worcestershire sauce

½ Pictsweet seasoning blend

1 tsp lemon juice

¼ cup Abita Amber beer (or other amber ale)

1 tsp dried parsley

2 cloves garlic, minced

1. Make the remoulade sauce by mixing all of the ingredients together thoroughly. Allow the sauce to sit in the refrigerator to let flavors meld for at least 1 hour.

2. Make fried pickles. Slice pickles into very thin slices.

3. In a bowl, whisk egg and whole milk together for batter.

4. On a plate, mix together flour, panko, and Tony Chachere's seasoning.

5. In a pan, heat vegetable oil to 350 degrees.

6. Batter pickles by dipping into dry mixture, then wet mixture and dropping into oil. Cook until golden brown, about 2-3 minutes per side. Place pickles on paper towel lined plate to catch excess oil.

7. Transfer to a platter and serve with remoulade sauce.

ABITA-CANE

Combining the classic New Orleans frozen-hurricane with the Louisiana-brewed Abita Beer. Makes 2 cocktails

INGREDIENTS:

2 ounces light rum

2 ounces dark rum

2 ounces pineapple juice

2 ounces orange juice

1 tbsp simple syrup

1 tbsp grenadine

1 12-ounce bottle Abita beer, or other amber ale

Ice

1. Mix ingredients, except the beer, together in blender until ice is blended smooth and preferred thickness is reached, adding more ice as necessary.

2. Pour into margarita glass.

3. Top with Abita beer and serve.

NEW YORK

THE BROOKLYN BEER PASTRAMI REUBEN

Submission by Tom Uddo

....

The "city that never sleeps" is the birthplace of pastrami, and what better way to celebrate New York and pastrami than combining it with a local favorite: the Brooklyn Brewery. The brewery, which was founded in 1987, features a selection of beers such as their lager, pilsner and pale ales, seasonal selections including their Winter and Summer Ales, as well as Dry Irish Stout and Oktoberfest. The hot sandwich features sliced New York pastrami, Russian dressing, Swiss cheese, and sauerkraut that is boiled in famous Brooklyn Beer Lager to give it a unique taste, all between toasted rye bread. This recipe truly combines the best of both worlds in terms of sandwiches and beer, two essentials on game day. Makes 1 large sandwich

....

INGREDIENTS:

2 tbsp Russian dressing

5 thin slices pastrami (about 4 ounces)

2 slices rye bread

1 cup sauerkraut

1 cup Brooklyn lager

2 slices Swiss cheese

1 tbsp unsalted butter, at room temperature

1. Add the sauerkraut to a sauce pan, and add one cup of Brooklyn lager. Cook over medium heat, simmering for 10-15 minutes, adding additional beer if needed to keep from drying out. Strain sauerkraut to drain excess liquid.

2. Spread one tbsp of Russian dressing on each slice of rye bread.

3. Place half of the pastrami, Swiss cheese, and Brooklyn Beer sauerkraut on each slice of the bread with the cheese directly on the bread (top and bottom when the sandwich is closed).

4. Press the sandwich firmly closed, and butter the top and bottom.

5. Heat a frying pan to medium heat and place the sandwich in the pan. Cook until the bread is golden brown on one side (about 4-5 minutes) and flip the sandwich to grill the other side, melting the cheese and heating up the insides.

6. Slice in half and serve.

PEPPERONI PIZZA BREAD

Pepperoni pizza bread is a personal favorite, but has always been a hidden recipe. For years my mother baked the dish and brought it to family parties, BBQ's, and dinners, with people asking her to spill the beans on how she does it. A thick layer of crust, stuffed with various cheeses, Italian pepperoni, and sausage, this appetizer would be on the menu in every Italian eatery in Little Italy. After weeks of coercion, my mother (who never seemed to understand the game of football), allowed me to dive into her recipe book, cracking the code on her pepperoni pizza for the world to enjoy on their football Sundays. Serves 6-10

INGREDIENTS:

1 package of pre-made pizza dough

¼ pound Genoa salami, sliced

¼ pound pepperoni, sliced

¼ pound provolone, sliced

2 cups shredded mozzarella cheese

1. Pre-heat an oven or grill to 400 degrees.

2. Roll out the dough in a rectangular shape and layer the ingredients alternating as follows: salami, provolone, pepperoni, and mozzarella.

3. Roll the dough with the ingredients like a jelly roll, making sure dough is tight, while pressing out the air bubbles.

4. Grease a cookie sheet lightly with olive oil and lay dough seam side down.

5. Brush lightly with oil and bake at 400 degrees until brown, 20-25 minutes.

Born and raised on Long Island, I still call the area my home at the age of 25. A die-hard New York Giants fan, I am proud to wear the colors of Big Blue. I may or may not have been contacted by Tom Brady and Bill Belichick on how to beat the Giants. My culinary "experience" ranges from some serious backyard BBQ-ing to tapping the keg and manning the bar on my deck during the hot summer nights in New York. Last year, I served as the Northeast Regional Correspondent for Stadium Journey and currently I am focusing my attention towards freelance journalism and web design. I have been featured on sites such as ESPN.com, Big Giants Boom, Long Island Politics, as well as various other sites.

-Tom Uddo

THE "LAWRENCE TAYLOR" ICED TEA

· ·

When looking up the definition of "linebacker" in the dictionary, there should be a picture of the Giants all-time great, Lawrence Taylor. Taylor is considered one of the best players to strap on a helmet in the pro football. Throughout his 13 year career, Taylor won two Super Bowls, was named an All-Pro six times and in 1999, he was inducted into the Hall of Fame. The "Lawrence Taylor" Iced Tea features all of the main ingredients of a traditional "Long Island Iced Tea," a cocktail that originated on Long Island, and adds a splash of Gatorade and blue curacao to reflect the colors that "LT" donned during his playing days as a New York Giant. Makes 1 cocktail

· ·

INGREDIENTS:

½ ounce triple sec

½ ounce gin

½ ounce rum

½ ounce vodka

½ ounce tequila

2 ounces red Gatorade

¼ ounce blue curacao

1 lemon wedge

1. In a cocktail shaker, add ice, vodka, gin, rum, triple sec , curacao, and tequila.

2. Fill a Collins glass with ice and strain mixture.

3. Top off drink with Gatorade.

4. Serve with a lemon wedge as garnish.

NEW YORK

REUBEN PIZZA

Submission by Kristen Merrill

....

As a New York deli staple, the Reuben translates to tailgating food when paired with that other classic New York food: pizza. Caraway seeded crust and the tang of sauerkraut create a familiar taste for New Yorkers who grew up on deli foods. If you want a slightly different taste, you can replace the corned beef with deli-sliced turkey for a Rachael Pizza. Makes 1 pizza, 4-8 servings

....

INGREDIENTS:

Pizza Dough (recipe makes enough dough for 2 pizzas, freeze the second batch for easier prep next time):

1 ¾ cups warm water

1 package (2 ¼ tsp) active dry yeast

2 tsp salt

4 ¾ cup bread flour

3 tbsp olive oil, plus more for bowl

Cornmeal for dusting pan

2 tbsp caraway seeds, divided

Pizza:

10 slices Swiss cheese

¾ cup sauerkraut

½ pound sliced corned beef (or sliced turkey)

½ cup mayonnaise

3 tbsp ketchup

2 tbsp sweet pickle relish

1 tbsp white vinegar

Pinch of salt and black pepper

1 tbsp olive oil

1. Prepare the dough. In a large bowl, sprinkle the yeast on top of the warm water. Allow it to bloom until foamy (about 5-10 minutes).

2. In the bowl of an electric mixer fitted with a dough hook, combine 2 cups of the flour and the salt.

3. Add the yeast mixture to the flour mixture and mix again.

4. Add the olive oil. Mix to combine.

5. Add the remaining flour, a little bit at a time, until the dough holds together. Add 1 tablespoon of the caraway seeds. Mix to combine. Knead the dough for 2-3 minutes until the dough begins to climb the dough hook.

6. Turn out the dough onto a floured surface and form into a ball.

7. Wipe down the bowl and coat the sides of the bowl lightly with olive oil. Place the dough back in the bowl. Cover with plastic wrap or a kitchen towel and allow to rise in a warm place for 45 minutes until doubled in size.

Continues on next page

8. While the dough is rising, make the thousand island dressing by combining mayonnaise, ketchup, sweet pickle relish, white vinegar, pinch of salt, and pinch of black pepper. Mix thoroughly. Set aside.

9. Pre-heat oven to 450 degrees.

10. Punch down the dough and divide into two halves. Freeze one dough ball if not using immediately.

11. Roll out the dough with a rolling pin or stretch with your hands. Dough should form a 12-inch pizza. Place stretched dough on either a cornmeal-dusted pizza stone or cookie sheet.

12. Spread half of the Thousand Island dressing on the dough, as you would a pizza sauce.

13. Cover with a thin layer of Swiss cheese slices.

14. Scatter the sauerkraut evenly around the pizza.

15. Place slices of corned beef (or turkey) evenly around the pizza.

16. Cover the meat with the remaining slices of Swiss cheese.

17. Lightly brush the edge of the crust with olive oil and sprinkle with salt and the remaining caraway seeds.

18. Bake for 18-20 minutes until golden brown.

19. Allow to cool for 5 minutes before slicing.

20. Drizzle remaining thousand island dressing on top of pizza after baking.

21. Cut into 8 slices and serve.

DIRTY WATER PRETZEL DOGS

Combining the classic staples of New York street food – hot dogs and soft pretzels – these Dirty Water Pretzel Dogs make the perfect tailgating snack. Serve with cold beer and spicy mustard and you're ready to cheer on the Jets wherever you are! Making the pretzel dough with beer instead of water lends a familiar malty flavor to the pretzels. Make it with Brooklyn Lager or another New York beer for even more regional taste!
Serves 18

INGREDIENTS:

18 hot dogs

1 bottle (12 ounces) beer

1 tbsp sugar

2 tsp kosher salt

1 package (2 ¼ teaspoons) active dry yeast

4 ½ cups bread flour

¼ cup unsalted butter, melted

1 large egg yolk

1 tbsp water

⅔ cup baking soda

¼ cup sea salt, or other large flaky salt

Spicy brown mustard

1. Allow the beer to come to room temperature before using. Once it reaches room temperature, combine the beer, sugar, and 2 teaspoons kosher salt in a small bowl. Sprinkle the yeast on top and allow to bloom for five minutes until the yeast is bubbling.

2. In a separate bowl, combine the bread flour and butter. If using an electric mixer, fit the mixer with a dough hook. Using the mixer, add the yeast mixture to the flour mixture and mix for 2-3 minutes until combined. If the dough is sticky, add additional flour, 1 tablespoon at a time, until the dough holds together and pulls away from the sides of the bowl. When the dough starts to climb the dough hook, dough is ready to rest. Remove dough hook and allow dough to rest, covered with a kitchen towel, for 30 minutes. The dough can also be made without a mixer. Use a wooden spoon or spatula to combine ingredients and knead by hand, on a floured surface.

3. Pre-heat oven or grill to 400 degrees.

4. Line two baking sheets with parchment paper or grease with butter.

5. Bring a large pot of water and baking soda to a boil while rolling out the dough.

6. Once the dough is rested, remove it from the bowl and place on a floured surface. Using a rolling pin, roll the dough out to approximately ⅛-inch thickness. Get the shape as close to rectangular as possible, trimming the edges if necessary.

7. Using a knife, cut the dough into 18 1-inch strips.

8. Using a spiral motion, wrap a strip of dough around each hot dog, pinching the ends to hold. If you prefer mini-dogs, cut each hot dog and each dough strip in half before wrapping and continue with smaller pieces.

9. Lay wrapped dogs on a plate until all pieces are wrapped. Depending on the temperature of the dough, chilling the wrapped dogs in the refrigerator may aid in the process.

10. Once all dogs are wrapped, drop them 2 or 3 at a time into the boiling water for 30 seconds each. Boiling the dough in the baking soda water will create the glossy, chewy pretzel exterior. Remove the dogs after 30 seconds and place on the lined baking sheet.

11. Once all dogs are placed on the baking sheets, beat together the egg yolk and 1 tablespoon of water. Lightly brush the dogs with the egg wash and sprinkle with the remaining sea salt or large flake salt.

12. Bake the dogs in the oven for 15 minutes, or until golden brown. If you prefer darker pretzels, allow to bake for an additional few minutes.

13. Serve with spicy brown mustard and cold beer.

NEW YORK STYLE APPLE CIDER SANDY SHANDY

Combining New York lager (Brooklyn Lager would be perfect) with regional apple cider lends a local twist to the classic shandy beverage. You can make this drink in individual servings or mix in larger pitchers to please a crowd! Makes 2 cocktails, or multiply for larger batch

INGREDIENTS:

1 bottle (12 ounces) Brooklyn lager, or other New York-style lager beer

12 ounces apple cider

1. Distribute lager between two chilled glasses.

2. Top with 6 ounces of apple cider in each glass.

3. Stir to combine.

OAKLAND

THE "MADDEN BOMBER"

Submission by Scott Kammerer

....

This colossal meal between bread should be at every Northern California tailgate party. The Golden State ranches and farms are well represented here with the tri-tip sirloin, mushrooms, onions and of course the mouth-watering California potato salad! Serves 6

....

INGREDIENTS:

Potato Salad:

1 ½ pounds Riverside red or Russet potatoes, quartered

1 tbsp Dijon mustard

¼ cup minced celery

¼ cup minced red onion

¼ Jamaican relish

Kosher salt

Freshly ground pepper

Continues on next page

INGREDIENTS (CONTINUED):

Tri-tip Beef:

2 ½ pounds tri-tip sirloin

3 tbsp ground onion powder

3 tbsp garlic powder

2 tbsp coarse kosher salt

1 tbsp fresh ground pepper

French roll

¼ cup melted butter

2 yellow or white onions, sliced

2 tbsp butter

½ pound sliced mushrooms

2 tsp dried oregano

½ cup beef broth

1 tbsp corn starch

1. Make the potato salad. Bring a large pot of water to a boil. Add potatoes and bring back to a boil. Cook quartered potatoes over medium low heat until soft, about 20 minutes. Drain and cool.

2. Mix with other potato salad ingredients and refrigerate overnight or at least two hours.

3. Heat grill on medium.

4. Prepare the steak by rubbing in the onion powder, garlic powder, salt, and pepper. Allow to sit at room temperature for about 20 minutes.

5. Place steak on the grill for 20 minutes, fat side up.

6. Place over indirect heat for another 20 minutes or until thermometer reads 130 degrees. Remove from heat and let rest for 10 minutes. Slice thin.

7. Sauté mushrooms in a little butter. Add mixture of broth, oregano, and corn starch. Stir until thickened.

8. Melt butter in a sauté pan over medium-high heat and sweat onions until tender.

9. Spread melted butter on the French roll and toast over direct heat on the grill.

10. Add an even layer of potato salad.

11. Top with four slices of the steak.

12. Add mushrooms and onions. Slice mammoth sandwich into individual portions and serve.

BO KNOWS MAC AND CHEESE

Bo Jackson's favorite meal growing up was Mac and Cheese. I believe this very creamy, smoked in a red pepper, two-step version would meet his approval. Serves 6

INGREDIENTS:

8 ounces elbow macaroni

12 ounces sharp cheddar cheese, grated

1 egg

1 cup milk

1 tsp hot English mustard

1 tsp white pepper

1 tsp coarse kosher salt

½ tsp Louisiana hot sauce

6 red bell peppers, tops removed and seeded

1. Bring water to a boil, and add the macaroni noodles, and salt. Boil until it is just tender according to package directions.

2. Drain thoroughly (DO NOT RINSE) and pour back in the same hot saucepan; mix in butter and melt.

3. Add the grated cheese and mix with the noodles.

4. In a medium bowl, whip the egg with the milk, mustard, white pepper, and hot sauce and pour into the macaroni mixture.

5. Fill peppers with hot mac and cheese. Place on grill over indirect heat and cook for about 30 minutes or until peppers soften. Place peppers over direct heat for 3-5 minutes to char slightly if desired.

THE LOOSE GANNON

Makes 6 cocktails

INGREDIENTS:

9 ounces silver tequila

3 ounces orange liqueur

1 pint of blackberries

1 ½ ounces cranberry juice

1 ½ ounces lime juice

3 tsp sugar

1. Divide blackberries into six glasses. Add ½ tsp of sugar into each glass and muddle lightly to release juices.

2. Fill with ice.

3. In a cocktail shaker, combine remaining ingredients and shake vigorously. Strain into the six glasses and serve.

PHILADELPHIA

CHEESE STEAK SAMMY

Submission by Anna Hopkins

. . . .

The classic Philly Cheesesteak. Makes 3 sandwiches

. . . .

INGREDIENTS:

1 ¼ pounds NY strip steak

1 tbsp salt

1 tsp black pepper

½ tsp paprika

1 tbsp Canola oil

5 tbsp butter

4 tbsp flour

1 ¼ cup warm milk

3 ounces provolone cheese

2 ounces pepper jack cheese

1 clove garlic

1 tbsp olive oil

Salt and pepper

½ yellow onion, julienned

2 dashes Worcestershire sauce

3 French rolls or hoagie buns

1. Rub steak with salt, pepper, and paprika. Refrigerate meat for 1 hour.

2. Using a very sharp knife, slice the steak as thinly as possible.

3. Prepare the cheese sauce by melting butter in saucepan. Once melted, add flour and whisk thoroughly until light brown mixture forms. Add warm milk and whisk until combined.

4. Once thickened slightly, add provolone and pepper jack cheese and melt until you have a cheese sauce. Add a pinch of salt and pepper to taste.

5. For the pepper garnish, heat a sauté pan with 1 tbsp butter. Once hot, add onions and salt. Allow onions to caramelize for 3-5 minutes. Add Worcestershire to the onion mixture. Add green peppers and sauté for 5-6 minutes.

6. Heat a large sauté pan with canola oil. Add meat to pan and flip each piece as it browns (2 minutes per side).

7. Once meat is cooked, take it off heat and allow it to rest for 5 minutes.

8. To assemble sandwiches, cut bread and spread some cheese sauce on the bottom of the bread. Pile meat on bread and drizzle more cheese sauce. Garnish with warm peppers and onions.

CREAM CHEESE AND CHORIZO STUFFED JALAPEÑOS

Crunchy jalapeños baked with a chorizo cream cheese and panko breading. Serves 2

INGREDIENTS:

5 jalapeños, cut lengthwise, seeds removed

8 ounces cream cheese

2 ounces, chorizo sausage

1 clove garlic

2 tbsp sour cream

8 chives, finely chopped

½ cup, shredded cheddar cheese

½ cup panko breadcrumbs

1. Pre-heat oven or grill to 350 degrees.

2. Heat a sauté pan and cook chorizo sausage over medium heat. Once cooked through, reduce to a low heat and add cream cheese and sour cream.

3. Chop garlic and add to cream cheese mixture. Add chives.

4. Once cream cheese mixture is well mixed, place halved peppers on a foil lined sheet tray. Spoon cream cheese into peppers. Top each pepper with shredded cheddar. Next top with panko.

5. Put peppers in the oven for 25 minutes or until breadcrumbs are golden brown.

MIDNIGHT GREEN MOJITO

Submission by Paul Swaney

Midnight green because it's the official uniform color of the Eagles. Makes 1 cocktail

INGREDIENTS:

5 mint leaves (in honor of Donovan McNabb, use 7 if you're more of a Ron Jaworski fan)

2 ounces white rum

2 ounces Midori

1 ounce simple syrup

Soda water

Mint sprig, for garnish

Ice

1. In a cocktail shaker, muddle the mint leaves and rum. If you have the time and patience, allow to sit for 15 minutes.

2. Add the Midori, simple syrup, and some ice. Shake and pour into a glass over additional ice.

3. Garnish with the mint sprig and top off with soda water.

PITTSBURGH

PIEROGI CASSEROLE

Submission by Joshua Guiher

A tailgate-friendly take on a Pittsburgh staple: pierogies. Serves 8

INGREDIENTS:

3 pounds potatoes

½ cup butter

½ cup sour cream

½ cup chopped onion

1 pound cheddar, shredded

12 lasagna noodles

1. Cook lasagna noodles until al dente according to package instructions, and drain.

2. In a pan, combine butter and onion and sauté for 20 minutes on low heat.

3. Peel, wash, and cut potatoes into ½-inch squares.

4. Boil potatoes until soft, approximately 20 minutes, drain.

5. Combine potatoes, sour cream, butter, and onion mixture; mash until creamy.

6. Layer in a 9x13 casserole dish using 3 lasagna noodles, ¼ of the mashed potato mixture, and ¼ pound of cheddar; repeating 4 times until all ingredients are used. Store in refrigerator until needed.

7. Bake at 400 degrees in oven or on grill until internal temperature reaches 365 degrees.

BLACK AND GOLD CORN

An extremely easy and tasty way to make corn-on-the-cob. Serves 8

INGREDIENTS:

8 ears of corn

½ cup melted butter

Salt and pepper

1. Carefully pull back husk (do not remove) and remove silk for each ear of corn.

2. Roll corn in melted butter; sprinkle with salt and pepper. Fold husk back into place.

3. Grill at 350 degrees for 20 minutes. Husk will blacken, but rotate every 5 minutes to prevent severe burning.

4. Peel off husk, add more butter, salt and pepper as desired.

STEEL CURTAIN COCKTAIL

A festive fall cocktail to wash down your Pittsburgh-themed food. Makes 1 cocktail

INGREDIENTS:

3 ounces Canadian Mist whiskey

3 ounces pear nectar

1 ounce peach nectar

1 ounce lime juice

1 slice of pear

1. Pour liquid ingredients into a cocktail shaker over ice and shake well.

2. Strain into a chilled cocktail glass.

3. Garnish with pear slice.

SAN DIEGO

TEQUILA-LIME GRILLED CHICKEN FAJITAS

Submission by Mike Becker

Chicken marinated in tequila and lime then grilled and sliced thin. It is topped with fire-roasted yellow, red, and green bell peppers and served with a side of citrus coleslaw. Serves 4

INGREDIENTS:

4 chicken breasts

1 bag coleslaw mix

¾ cup lime juice

3 ounces tequila

1 jalapeño pepper, chopped

10 leaves cilantro

1 tbsp sugar

⅛ tsp salt

⅛ tsp pepper

1 green pepper

1 yellow pepper

1 red pepper

8 flour tortillas

1. Place chicken, ½ cup of lime juice, tequila, and chopped jalapeño in a plastic bag and refrigerate for one hour.

2. While chicken marinates, begin by fire roasting your peppers. The peppers should be black on all sides, and after the peppers are black, place them in a plastic or brown paper bag to cool. This makes it easier to remove the skin.

3. Combine coleslaw mix with the remaining lime juice, salt, and pepper, toss together and adjust seasoning if needed.

4. Remove the chicken from the bag, transfer to a dish, and place on pre-heated grill.

5. Grill the chicken for about 5 minutes, then flip and cook for an additional 5 minutes.

6. While the chicken is grilling, take the peppers from the bag and use the back of a knife to scrape the black skin off.

7. Cut the peppers in half lengthwise and remove all the seeds and inner membrane, then julienne the peppers.

8. To assemble the fajitas, place chicken in the bottom of a tortilla then top with the peppers and coleslaw.

GRILLED OYSTER TRIO

Oysters grilled on the half shell and topped with 3 unique toppings. Serves 4

INGREDIENTS:

12 large oysters

Corn Salsa:

1 ear of corn, grilled and sliced off the cob

1 tbsp habanero pepper, minced

1 tbsp lime juice

½ cup diced tomato

Salt and pepper to taste

Yellow Pepper Chutney:

1 yellow pepper, diced

1 medium onion, diced

2 cloves garlic, minced

1 tsp minced jalapeño

⅙ cup sugar

⅙ cup apple cider vinegar

¾ tbsp. pineapple juice

⅛ tsp salt

Grilled Pineapple Salsa:

4 pineapple rings, grilled

½ cup red onion, diced

1 tbsp jalapeño pepper, minced

1 tbsp lime juice

1. Make the yellow pepper chutney. Combine all the ingredients for the yellow pepper chutney in a small sauce pot and simmer on low heat until the peppers are tender, stirring occasionally.

2. Grill the ear of corn and combine with other ingredients to make corn salsa.

3. Grill the pineapple rings on medium heat until warmed through and char marks appear. Chop small and combine with other ingredients to make pineapple salsa.

4. Heat your grill and place the oyster halves shell-side-down and grill for about 5 minutes. Top oysters with the trio of salsas, serving one of each to each guest.

ELECTRIC LEMONADE

Refreshing summer drink served in a tall glass with lots of ice. Makes 1 cocktail

INGREDIENTS:

3 ounces vodka

1 ½ ounces lemon simple syrup (⅔ cup sugar and ¼ cup lemon juice)

1 ounce blue curacao

Splash of club soda

Lemon slice for garnish

1. Combine ice, simple syrup, vodka, and the blue curacao in a cocktail shaker.

2. Shake well, ensuring drink is thoroughly chilled.

3. Fill a highball glass with ice and pour the drink in the glass.

4. Top off the glass with splash of club soda.

5. Garnish with lemon slice and serve.

SAN FRANCISCO

49 CLOVE GARLIC CHICKEN

Submission by Paul Swaney

If you have never learned a trick for peeling garlic quickly, then this will be the time to learn. Whether you use the chef knife smash, or the two metal bowl shake, you'll want to have a trick ready to make prep time easier. You can cook this in a stove if at home or on a grill. If using a gas grill with two burners, then you should only light one side and cook on the unlit side. If you have three burners, then keep the middle burner unlit and cook there. If using a charcoal grill, then keep coals on one side and cook on the opposite. The key is to achieve a temperature when covered of about 400 degrees. Serves 4-6

INGREDIENTS:

1 whole chicken (4-5 pounds)

49 cloves of garlic (about 4-5 heads)

Salt and pepper

1 lemon, halved

Sourdough bread

3 tbsp olive oil

1. Light a grill as described above, or pre-heat the oven to 400 degrees.

2. Peel the garlic and set aside.

3. Rinse the chicken and then pat dry thoroughly. The key to juicy chicken is a dry bird when you begin roasting.

4. Stuff all of the garlic in the chicken, and then truss the legs to ensure the garlic does not fall out. Season generously with salt and pepper.

5. Place in oven or grill breast side down, and cook for 45 minutes.

6. If grilling, flip the chicken and cook for an additional 35-45 minutes.

7. Remove chicken and let rest on a cutting board for about 10 minutes before carving.

8. Meanwhile, remove the cloves of garlic. You should be able to mash with a fork, but if they are not yet soft enough, then pop in the microwave for 1-2 minutes. Add the oil and a sprinkle of salt and pepper and mash into a paste (alternatively you can use a food processor). Serve with sourdough bread or spread on chicken when serving.

9. Place the lemon on the heated part of the grill and cook for 5-6 minutes. Use the juice as a sauce for the chicken, or mix in with the garlic paste for another great flavor component.

ZUCCHINI CARPACCIO

. . . .

This light and bright salad is the perfect complement to the chicken, and easy to prepare. You can use either yellow squash or zucchini or a mix of the two. You can also substitute any leafy fresh herb for the basil if you like (arugula works great, but you could also try dandelion greens, parsley, baby spinach, or sage). Serves 6

. . . .

INGREDIENTS:

1 pound of baby zucchini or yellow squash. Look for vegetables that are as skinny as possible.

½ lemon, juiced

3 tbsp olive oil

Salt and pepper

⅓ tsp dried oregano

6 basil leaves, cut into ribbons

Parmesan cheese, shaved for garnish (or another hard cheese like Pecorino Romano would work as well)

1. Chop off the top end of the squash, and using a vegetable peeler, slice circular pieces into a bowl, rotating the squash as you do it to ensure that you maintain a flat surface for peeling.

2. In a small Tupperware container, combine the lemon juice, olive oil, oregano, and season with salt and pepper. Shake well and the pour over squash, mixing with your hands or tongs.

3. Arrange squash pieces on a plate in a circular fashion, or if you're in a rush, just toss in a bowl. Sprinkle on some black pepper, the basil, and shave some parmesan cheese on top. Enjoy!

THE MINER FORTY-NINER

. . . .

The colder it gets, the better this cinnamon-flavored drink gets. Makes 1 cocktail

. . . .

INGREDIENTS:

2 ounces of Goldschlager

½ ounce grenadine (1 tbsp)

¼ tsp lemon zest

Slice of lemon

7up

1. Fill a tumbler with ice.

2. Add Goldschlager, grenadine, and lemon zest.

3. Add a slice of lemon to the side of the glass.

4. Top glass with 7up.

SEATTLE

SEATTLE SALMON

Submission by Joshua Guiher

An extremely tasty salmon recipe that is also extremely easy to make. Serves 8

INGREDIENTS:

8 8-ounce salmon fillets

4 cedar planks

½ cup vegetable oil

2 tbsp rice wine vinegar

½ cup soy sauce

½ cup green onions, chopped

2 tbsp ginger root, grated

¼ cup minced garlic (about 10-12 cloves)

¼ cup honey

8 thin orange slices

1. Soak cedar planks in cold water for one hour.

2. Meanwhile, in a casserole pan, combine vegetable oil, rice wine vinegar, soy sauce, chopped green onions, ginger root, garlic, and honey and whisk for 2-3 minutes.

3. Place salmon face down in sauce and marinate for 45 minutes.

4. Place 2 salmon fillets skin down on each cedar plank and grill until it flakes with a fork, approximately 20 minutes at 300 degrees.

5. Garnish with orange slices.

SPACE NEEDLE ASPARAGUS

A simple tailgating take on asparagus. Serves 8

INGREDIENTS:

1 pound asparagus

¼ tsp salt

¼ tsp black pepper

Olive oil

1. Grill Asparagus at 300 degrees for approximately 20 minutes, rotating every few minutes.

2. Season with salt and pepper, drizzle with olive oil, and serve.

HONEY IRISH ALE

This honey whiskey and ginger ale cocktail will be the perfect complement to your cedar plank salmon. Makes 1 cocktail

INGREDIENTS:

2 ounces honey whiskey

3 ounces ginger ale

3 lime wedges

1. Pour honey whiskey and ginger ale into a Collins glass.

2. Squeeze two lime wedges into drink and stir.

3. Top off with ice and garnish with remaining lime wedge.

ST. LOUIS

ST. LOUIS PORK STEAKS

Submission by John Dawson

St. Louis pork steaks are "steaks" that are cut from a pork butt. They are typically seared over a hot charcoal fire and then braised in a mixture of beer and BBQ sauce. How can you possibly go wrong with that? These are really simple, but the results are spectacular. I use a basic "Dalmatian" (salt and pepper) seasoning with a little garlic. I'd urge those of you that are BBQ masters to resist the urge to over-complicate things by adding a bunch of extra ingredients. You want steaks that are cut at least an inch thick, but I prefer 1 ¼-inch. If you can't find them in the case at your local store (they're typically labeled as "blade steaks"), just ask the butcher to cut some from a pork butt. Serves 6

INGREDIENTS:

4 large pork steaks 1 ¼-inch thick

3 tbsp kosher salt

1 ½ tbsp black pepper

2 tsp granulated garlic

16 ounces light beer

18 ounces of your favorite BBQ sauce

Note: You'll also need two 9-13 disposable aluminum roaster pans

1. Combine the salt, pepper, and garlic in a small bowl and mix well.

2. Season both sides of each steak liberally with the seasoning, then place them in zip-top bags and refrigerate at least three hours or overnight.

3. Start your grill and prepare for direct cooking over high heat (450-500 degrees). Sear the steaks on each side.

4. While the steaks are searing, combine the beer and BBQ sauce in a large bowl and whisk to combine.

5. Put the steaks in a single layer into the disposable aluminum pans and cover them with the beer mixture, putting half of the beer and BBQ sauce mixture into each pan.

6. Cover the pans tightly with foil.

7. Move your coals to one side of the grill for indirect cooking. Put the pans on the side of the grill opposite the coals and cook, indirect, for 90 minutes. Add charcoal as needed to keep the temperature at about 350 degrees throughout the rest of the cooking time.

8. Remove the steaks from the pans and quickly sear them over direct heat (about 2 minutes per side). Remove to a platter and let rest for about five minutes.

9. Slice and enjoy!

GRILLED CHICKEN TOASTED RAVIOLI

. . . .

Here is my take on classic St. Louis toasted ravioli. I've added a grilled twist that really works well in the filling. I don't know why these pillows of fried pasta goodness are called "toasted," but I do know that they are very good. I'm sure that there are some purists out there reading this and thinking, "Wonton wrappers, what the...?! What a pathetic, lazy excuse for pasta!" I understand that it's clearly not traditional. If you like spending the time and having every horizontal surface of your kitchen covered with a dusting of flour, go for it. I'm going the lazy route. Come on, try it, I won't tell anyone. Serves 4

. . . .

INGREDIENTS:

½ cup grilled chicken, finely chopped

¼ cup frozen chopped spinach, thawed and squeezed dry

¼ cup shredded pepper jack cheese

3 tbsp crimini mushrooms, finely chopped

1 scallion, finely chopped

1 egg

1 tbsp water

12-14 wonton wrappers

¾ cup Italian-style breadcrumbs

4 cups peanut oil or Canola oil

1 tbsp parmesan cheese, grated

Marinara sauce for dipping

1. Combine the chicken, spinach, pepper jack, mushrooms, and scallion in a medium mixing bowl and stir well to combine.

2. Heat the frying oil in a large heavy pot (I recommend cast iron) to 360 degrees.

3. Whisk the egg and water together in a small bowl.

4. Brush the outer edge of a wonton wrapper with the egg wash, add about a tablespoon of the filling to the center, fold carefully, and pinch the edge to seal it. Make sure that it's sealed completely. Repeat with the remaining wrappers and filling.

5. Working in batches of four or five, brush all sides of each ravioli with the egg wash (or dip them), coat each completely with bread crumbs, and carefully drop them into the oil, waiting a couple of seconds between each. Fry the ravioli until they are golden brown. Remove to a wire rack inside a lipped sheet pan that's lined with several layers of paper towels.

6. Plate, sprinkle with parmesan, and serve with the marinara sauce for dipping.

SHANDY COOLER

Makes 1 cocktail

INGREDIENTS:

8 ounces unfiltered wheat ale (like Shock Top Belgian White)

2 slices of lemon

1 ½ ounces vodka

6 ounces ginger ale

1. Muddle one slice of lemon and vodka, strain into a 16-ounce pub glass, add the beer and ginger ale.

2. Serve garnished with slice of lemon.

I am a husband, the father of three young girls, an Air Force veteran, and a cook living in Boise, Idaho.

By day I am a senior software engineer specializing in web user interfaces. As for BBQ, I've been competing in BBQ competitions since 2006 under the name "Patio Daddio BBQ".

As for cooking in general, my passion is good hearty rustic food. I often say that life is too short to eat mediocre food. It may sound corny, but food to me is a way of giving a little of myself to those I cook for. It's a gift on a plate. There are few things in life more intimate than sharing a meal. I am also an artist, so cooking is a natural creative outlet for me.

-John Dawson

TAMPA BAY

ORANGE GRILLED SHRIMP

Submission by Paul Swaney

Gulf shrimp are perfect for this dish in order to keep it regional, but larger tiger shrimp are delicious as well. Just go for what looks good and keeps your prep to a minimum. Serves 4

INGREDIENTS:

1 pound deveined and shelled shrimp, tail-on

1 large orange

2 cloves garlic, minced

6 sage leaves, minced (or other fresh herb such as tarragon, parsley, oregano, or mint)

¼ tsp coriander

¼ tsp black pepper

¼ tsp salt

Olive oil

1. In a shallow dish, place shrimp in a single layer.

2. Zest the orange and sprinkle over shrimp.

3. Cut the orange in half and juice one half, pouring over the shrimp (about 1/3 cup). Reserve other half of orange for grilling.

4. Add other ingredients and marinate in refrigerator for one hour.

5. Pre-heat grill over medium heat, applying light olive oil to grates. Add shrimp and grill for about 3-4 minutes per side, turning as soon as grill side begins to look pink. Exact cooking time will depend on size of shrimp. Place reserved half of orange on grill as well.

6. Pull shrimp from the grill and place on a plate. Using tongs, take the orange off the grill and squeeze juice over shrimp. Drizzle with olive oil and serve.

STUFFED BELL PEPPERS

Florida produces almost 50% of all of the bell peppers consumed in the United States. This versatile recipe is a great way to use up leftover vegetables and can be stuffed with any kind of ground meat, or substitute rice for a vegetarian option. Serves 4

INGREDIENTS:

2 bell pepper (orange or red)

½ pound ground hamburger (or other ground meat of your choice)

1 cup carrot, chopped

1 cup zucchini, chopped

½ cup onion, chopped

4 slices cheddar cheese

Fresh parsley, chopped for garnish

Salt and pepper

1. Pre-heat oven or grill to 400 degrees.

2. Slice bell peppers in half and remove seeds and membrane. Place in a shallow baking dish and rub olive oil all over. If grilling, place peppers on the top rack, away from the flames and cook for 15-20 minutes. In the oven, roast for 20 minutes in center of oven.

3. Meanwhile, brown meat in a pan over medium heat, adding olive oil if necessary. Once the meat is browned, remove to a paper towel.

4. Add carrots to pan, adding more olive oil if necessary. Cook for 5 minutes. Add in zucchini and onion and cook for an additional 5 minutes. Combine with ground meat.

5. Pull peppers from the oven and stuff with meat and vegetable mixture. Bake for 15 minutes. If grilling, keep on upper shelf of grill.

6. Add sliced cheese on top of peppers and bake for an additional 5 minutes.

7. Sprinkle with parsley and serve.

GRAPEFRUIT MOJITO

In March, I think of the Grapefruit League when I think of Florida. Come September, the fruit helps to provide a Central Florida twist on a South Florida favorite. Makes 3 cocktails

INGREDIENTS:

1 cup white rum

½ cup white sugar

½ cup water

8 sprigs mint

1 ruby red grapefruit

Seltzer water

1. Peel rind off grapefruit using vegetable peeler and place in measuring cup. Add one cup of rum and let it flavor for 30-60 minutes.

2. On a stovetop or grill, combine sugar and water and cook over low heat until sugar dissolves, forming a simple syrup. Add 4 springs of mint to syrup, remove from heat, and let sit for 15 minutes (can be made a day ahead).

3. Cut pith away from the grapefruit and cut into segments. Place 3 segments in each glass.

4. Remove mint springs from syrup and place at the bottom of each glass, muddling slightly. Add ice.

5. In a cocktail shaker, combine rum, and 2/3 cup of simple syrup. Pour in even amounts into each glass.

6. Top each glass with a little bit of seltzer water. Add a mint sprig for garnish. Stir well.

7. If you have extra pieces of grapefruit, you can juice into the glass for extra grapefruit flavor (optional).

TENNESSEE

PORKY NACHOS

Submission by Anna Hopkins

Salty tortilla chips with tender pulled pork and you choice of garnishes. Meaty, cheesy, and delicious! Serves 6

INGREDIENTS:

½ cup dry rub

2-3 pounds bone-in pork butt

1 ½ cups milk

2 ounces butter

2 ounces flour

1 cup sharp cheddar cheese, shredded

4 ounces cream cheese

Salt and pepper

Garnishes such as chopped green onion, sliced black olives, and avocado slices

Tortilla chips for serving

Additional Materials:

Charcoal

Hickory smoking chips

Aluminum foil

Charcoal starter barrel

1. Make the dry rub and rub all over pork butt. Refrigerate overnight, at least 12 hours.

2. On game day, prepare the smoker (see page 31 for instructions).

3. Smoke pork on opposite side of wood chips with vent half open.

4. Check on pork every 30-40 minutes to maintain temperature control. If the temperature is too low, add more hot coals using your barrel starter. Temperature should be 215-260 degrees.

5. After about 3 hours, remove pork from grill. If the meat is still slightly tough (not easily pulled apart), transfer your pork to the stove top. Simmer in some beef stock (pork half submerged) on medium to low heat for up to an hour or until tender enough to pull apart. Once your pork is ready, allow to rest for 15-20 minutes then pull apart for your nachos.

6. Prepare your cheese sauce. Warm the milk on a stovetop or microwave. Be careful not to boil.

7. Heat butter in medium size pot. Add flour and stir until combined.

8. Whisk in warm milk and allow mixture to thicken slightly (low heat).

9. Add the cheddar and cream cheese and stir until melted. Add salt and pepper.

10. Assemble nachos by plating tortilla chips and pulled pork on top. Dress with the warm cheese sauce and whatever garnishes you'd like.

GARLICKY GUACAMOLE

Creamy guacamole that is tasty with tortilla chips or fresh cut vegetables. Pairs well with Porky Nachos above. Serves 6

INGREDIENTS:

3 ripe avocadoes

3 tomatoes, seeded and diced

½ white onion, finely chopped

3 cloves garlic, toasted and mashed

1 jalapeño, seeds removed depending on level of heat desired, finely chopped

2 limes, juiced

1 tbsp salt

½ bunch cilantro, chopped

1. Prepare vegetables. Peel avocadoes and place into a large bowl. Add a pinch of salt and half of the lime juice. Mash until creamy.

2. Toast garlic cloves in a pan on the stove (skin on), rotate the clove so each side is browned. Once toasted, bring to your board and carefully smash with your knife. Remove skin and run your knife through garlic. Add a pinch of salt and using the width of your knife, push garlic across board, back and forth until smooth. Add garlic to avocado mixture.

3. In a medium bowl, mix the tomatoes, onion, and jalapeño together. Add the tomato mixture to the avocado mixture. Mix remaining lime juice in gently. Add salt and chopped cilantro.

4. Serve with tortilla chips, vegetables, or Garlicky Nachos.

LYNCHY SPRITZ

Inspired by a local favorite, the Lynchburg Lemonade, this cocktail is both refreshing and easy! Makes 1 cocktail

INGREDIENTS:

2 ounces Jack Daniels whiskey

1 ounce triple sec

2 ounces lemonade

2 ounces seltzer water

1 orange wedge, squeezed

1 lemon wedge, squeezed

1 lime wedge, squeezed

1. Chill a tall glass, and fill with large ice cubes.

2. Measure your ingredients and pour into glass in order listed. Gently pour so that the beverage appears layered and then can be mixed with a straw upon serving.

3. The garnishes and juice can be put in last. Serve with a straw.

WASHINGTON, DC

THE HOGS SANDWICH

By Paul Swaney

Jeff Bostic, Russ Grimm, and Joe Jacoby were the heart and soul of the offensive line of the Washington Redskins during their three Super Bowl victories in 1982, 1987, and 1991. This meaty sandwich pays homage to those underappreciated Redskins with a combination of pulled pork, ham, and bacon. The pulled pork will take about one hour per pound to cook, so plan accordingly by starting when you wake up, or perhaps overnight.

INGREDIENTS:

4 -6 pounds pork shoulder, bone-in preferred

1 pound thick cut bacon

1 pound sliced ham

1 pound sliced Swiss cheese

8 Kaiser rolls

2 cloves garlic

Olive oil

Stone ground mustard (or spicy brown mustard)

Pickled red onion (see recipe below)

RUB:

1 tsp ground black pepper

¼ tsp cayenne pepper

1 ½ tsp paprika

1 tbsp dried parsley flakes

1 tbsp dried thyme

1 tbsp smoked salt (or coarse salt as a substitute)

½ tsp white pepper

½ tsp garlic powder

½ tsp chili powder

½ tsp onion powder

Pickled Red Onion:

1 medium red onion, very thinly sliced

1 bay leaf

1 tsp whole peppercorns

½ tsp whole coriander

½ tsp dried thyme

½ cup red wine vinegar

1 cup cold water

1. Add sliced red onions to a pickling jar. Add spices and vinegar, and add enough water to cover. Refrigerate overnight.

2. Add all of the ingredients for the rub in a bowl, mixing well. Rub all over the pork shoulder until it is covered. Cook in a crock pot fatty side down on high for approximately one hour per pound. The bone should be able to be extracted cleanly when the pork is ready.

3. Shred the pork using tongs and a fork.

4. Cook the bacon.

Continues on next page

5. On a small plate, scatter the minced garlic and then cover with olive oil. Slice the Kaiser rolls and dredge or brush the cut side in the oil, adding more garlic and oil as needed.

6. Cook rolls on a grill, cut-side down only, or in a skillet over medium heat for about 2 minutes.

7. After removing rolls from heat, immediately place one slice of Swiss cheese on both the top and bottom of the roll so that they begin to melt.

8. Place a slice of ham on each piece of cheese.

9. On one side of the sandwich, place two slices of bacon. On the other side of the sandwich, place a good portion of the pulled pork.

10. Cover the pork with stone ground mustard. Top with pickled red onion.

11. Combine the two sides of the sandwich and enjoy!

RED GIN RICKEY

....

A classic DC cocktail gets a tinge of red by adding a muddled strawberry. It's easy and refreshing. Makes 1 cocktail

....

INGREDIENTS:

1 strawberry, top removed

¼ cup gin

1 lime

Sparkling water

Ice

1. Place strawberry in a tumbler glass and muddle with a spoon. Add ice.

2. Add the gin.

3. Slice the top off of a lime, and use the top as a garnish. With the remaining lime, juice it and add to the cocktail.

4. Top with sparkling water and serve.

ROASTED REDSKIN POTATOES WITH MUSTARD

Serves 4

....

This easy-to-assemble side dish could be done at home or at the tailgate. Just make sure you have something to roast the potatoes on if cooking on the grill like a grill basket.

....

INGREDIENTS:

⅓ cup Dijon mustard (don't use mustard with large seeds or they will burn when baking)

3 cloves garlic, chopped

1 tbsp olive oil

¼ stick of butter, melted

1 lemon, juiced (about 2 tbsp)

1 tsp dried oregano

1 tsp dried parsley flakes

½ tsp pepper

½ tsp salt

1 tbsp hot sauce (optional)

1 pound redskin potatoes, cut into bite sized pieces, with skin on

Cooking spray or additional olive oil

1. Pre-heat oven or grill to 425 degrees.

2. In a large bowl, combine all of the ingredients, except the potatoes, and stir.

3. Add in potatoes and toss to coat.

4. Apply cooking spray or olive oil to cooking sheet or grill basket.

5. Spread potatoes evenly on the cooking sheet, being careful not to pour excess marinade on the pan (excess marinade is great on chicken or lamb if you're grilling, or reserve excess sauce for potatoes once they are cooked).

6. Cook about 20 minutes. Check and turn potatoes. Cook another 10-15 minutes or until fork tender. Cover with excess sauce if desired.

RECIPE INDEX

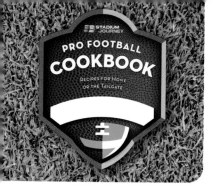

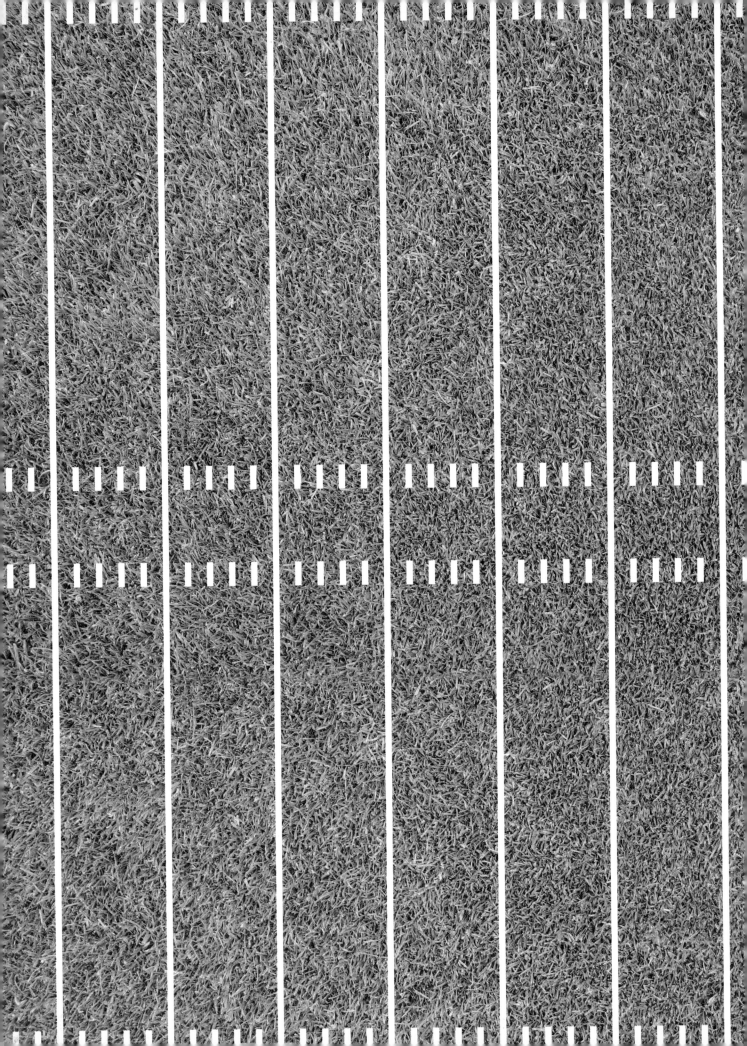